ART SHRINES OF ANCIENT INDIA

Books by V.K. Subramanian

The Great Ones

The Upanishads and the Bible

Introspection for India—A Paradigm for Progress

Sacred Songs of India (Volumes I, II, III, IV, V, VI, VII, VIII)

The Holistic Way to Health, Happiness and Harmony

Wondrous Whispers of Wisdom from Ancient India (Vols. I & II)

Predictive Planets and Presaging Palms

Maxims of Chanakya

Saundaryalahari

Sivanandalahari

Sri Rudraprasna

The Indian Financial System

Lali and Other Short Stories

Love Twigs

A Bond to Sorrow

ART SHRINES OF ANCIENT INDIA

V.K. Subramanian

ABHINAV PUBLICATIONS

abhinav publications

First published in India 2003

Publishers
Shakti Malik
Abhinav Publications
E-37 Hauz Khas
New Delhi-110016 (INDIA)
Phones: 26566387, 26562784, 26524658
Fax: 91-11-26857009
e-mail: shakti@nde.vsnl.net.in
website: http://www.abhinavexports.com

ISBN 81-7017-431-7

Phototypesetting in Bhaskerville 12 pt
and Processing by
Onkar Digital Studio
Rohini, Delhi-110085

Printed at
D.K. Fine Art Press Pvt. Ltd.
Ashok Vihar, Delhi

To

Shakti Malik, my Publisher
whose readiness to publish what I write
gives motivational momentum to my writing

Contents

Appendices

Preface

This book is, by and large, a compendium of articles written by me for the Bhavan's Journal.

Between 1976 and 1980, I happened to be the Director, I.A.A.S., Staff College, Simla in India and one of the pleasant duties I had to perform was to take my trainee-officers every year on a two-week tour of India. This was called *Bharat Darshan* or seeing India, especially places of important historical, artistic and archaeological significance.

During a five-year period, I had the opportunity to visit, along with my officers, the places covered in this book. Though most of the major Art Shrines could be covered, I must admit that there are important places which I could not visit and hence could not deal with in this book on Art Shrines of India.

Hence at best what I offer is only a sampling of India's glorious artistic heritage and I apologize for the incompleteness and the glaring omissions of places of major artistic significance.

But I consider myself lucky in having been able to travel and see and admire ancient India's artistic heritage—a privilege very few would get.

So, I offer my readers my incomplete sampling of India's ancient Art Shrines, which are still available for a visit and aesthetic appreciation.

Minneapolis, U.S.A. V.K. Subramanian

Acknowledgements

I am grateful to the Editors of Bhavan's Journal, Indrama (of Sita World Travel Service) and Travel Times, Times of India for kindly permitting me to use in book form some of the articles published in their journals.

I would like to thank Smt. Indira S. Aiyar, Mumbai, for kindly making available the photographs taken by her late husband, Sri Shankar Aiyar.

I am also indebted to my dear friend Late Sri R. Swaminathan, who so lovingly typed out the MSS.

V.K. Subramanian

Rough Location of Temples and Archaeological Sites dealt with in this Book

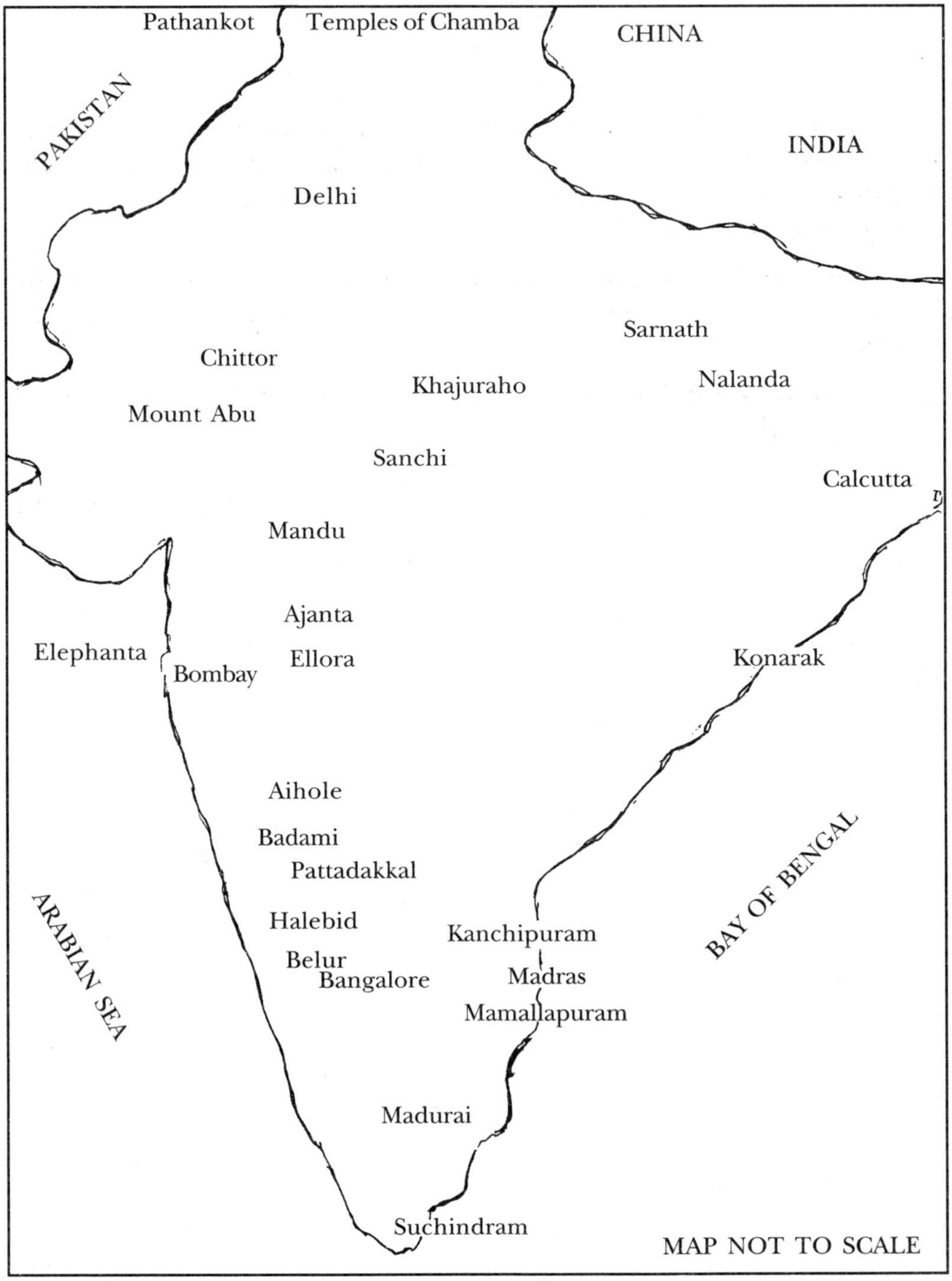

I

Introduction

Indian Art Through the Ages

Unity, variety and continuity mark Indian Art through the ages. From 3000 years before Christ to the twentieth century, Indian creative genius has sought and found expression in virtually imperishable stone and metal, as also in perishable wood and clay.

Despite the ravages of time and the vandalism of invaders and iconoclasts, the mementos of Indian creative expression have survived obscurity and oblivion.

We are grateful to a large number of devoted Englishmen like Cunningham, Fergusson, Hegel and Garrett for discovering our heritage in ruins and to leading historians and art critics of the West like Zimmer and Durant, Willets and Goetze for enabling us to understand the greatness of our ancient art and the invaluable contribution it has made to human civilization.

But, however earnest and erudite may be the efforts of foreigners to understand the meaning and method of Indian artistic heritage, only Indians can understand the soul and spirit behind it. To quote the famous American writer, Mark Twain: "A foreigner can photograph the exteriors of a nation, but I think that is as far as he can get. No foreigner can report its interior, its soul, its life, its speech, its thought."

Emboldened by Mark Twain's dictum, let us try to unravel the mysteries of the artistic legacy bequeathed to us by our ancestors during the 5000 years of our colourful and chequered history.

The first questions which naturally arise are: What are the great periods of Indian art? And where are the main places of pilgrimage where one can have a glimpse of the great achievements of Indian artists, architects, sculptors and craftsmen?

The great periods of Indian art are well known:

The Indus Valley Civilization; The Maurya Period; The Sunga Period; The art of the Kushanas; The early and later Andhra achievements; The golden age of the Guptas; The period of the Dravidian dynasties; The Chalukyas; The Pallavas; The Rashtrakutas; The Cholas; The Hoysalas; The Pandyas; The Northern and Eastern Hindu dynasties (Palas, Senas, Chandellas, etc.); The Nayaks; The Vijayanagar Empire; and the Mughal Period.

The main archaeological sites which enable us to have a peep into the past are given below statewise:

Andhra Pradesh: Amaravati, Nagarjunakonda, Lepakshi, Sivasailam and Warangal.

Bihar: Nalanda and Bodhgaya.

Himachal Pradesh: Chamba, Brahmour and Kulu Valley.

Jammu & Kashmir: Avantipur and Martand.

Kerala: Trivandrum, Ettumanoor, Mattancheri, Trichur, Virinjam, Irinjalakuda and Kaviyur.

Madhya Pradesh: Sanchi, Bharhut, Khajuraho, Vidisha, Mandu and Ujjain.

Maharashtra: Elephanta, Ajanta, Ellora, Bhaja & Karle Caves, Nasik, Aurangabad and Daulatabad.

Karnataka: Aihole, Badami, Belur, Halebid, Hampi, Pattadakkal, Somnathpur and Sravanabelagola.

Orissa: Konarak, Bhuvaneshwar, Khandagiri and Udayagiri Caves.

Rajasthan: Chittor, Mount Abu, Ranakpur, Abaneri, Ajmer, Jaipur, Udaipur, Jodhpur, Bikaner and Jaisalmer.

Tamil Nadu: Kanchipuram, Mahabalipuram, Chidambaram, Darasuram, Gangaikondacholapuram, Kumbakonam, Suchindram, Madurai, Thanjavur, Srirangam, Tiruchirapalli, Tiruvannamalai, Uttiramerur, Vellore and Parur.

Uttar Pradesh: Sarnath, Mathura, Agra, Fatehpur Sikri and Delhi.

What has been given is only an illustrative list of the most important places, which a tourist, short of time, would need to visit, to acquaint himself with the marvels of Indian achievement in the fields of architecture, sculpture and painting.

The table at page 18 summarises the various periods of Indian art, indicating the approximate dates and linking them with important tourist places, where the artistic creations can be seen. Sculpture and Architecture map on page 12 gives an idea of the locations of the important monuments.

It would be relevant at this stage to refer to some of the comments made by western critics on Indian art, expecially its most important forms:

The *Encyclopaedia Britannica* refers to Indian art as "theological or traditional", "since, like the art of the middle ages in Europe, it was dedicated to revealing the divine nature of the gods and enhancing the dignity of the Church." It adds: "Its didactic purpose was to instruct men in the truths of religion."

The late Will Durant wrote in his *Story of Civilisation*, Volume One, *The Oriental Heritage*, "The sculpture in India never quite acquired the grace of her literature or the sublimity of her architecture, or the depth of her philosophy, it mirrored chiefly the confused and uncertain insight of her religions."

While on the one hand, Indian art has been criticised as *Hieratic Art*—"devoted to the exposition of the personalities and acts of deities and providing for their service", that it has not been produced for aesthetic experience, that its themes are "dogmatic and mythological forms unparalleled in nature", several others have found objection to the earthy eroticism in Indian sculpture, pointing out that such expression arose out of depraved cults and practices.

When one reads and ponders over such ill informed and superficial understanding of Indian art, one has to pay tribute to the wisdom of Mark Twain and set the record straight.

In India, religion is not something divorced from life. *Synthesis of the spiritual and the sensual is a cardinal cornerstone of the Indian approach to art.* The creative genius of India has found its untrammelled outpouring in stone and metal and attained the zenith of excellence, in diverse periods of history, during the reigns of rulers vastly differing in their customs and religious beliefs.

The Jain temples in Dilwara in Mount Abu, the immortal Taj Mahal and the monuments in Fatehpur Sikri, the Buddhist paintings of Ajanta and the sculptural marvels of Elephanta and Ellora, the majestic marvels of the Chola period are all expressions of the same creative genius which is universal in character and represents art in its most genuine form.

The great Kalidasa said: "One who is not a Rishi cannot create art" (*Naanrshi kurutė kāvyam*). The wise Socrates said 2000 years ago: "Creativity has its origin in the divine element in man." It is true that in India, all art is God-oriented, and God is seen and eulogised in every facet of manifest creation. That is why the Indian sculptor pays glorious tributes, with his chisel and hammer, to the human form, both male and female and idealising it, also reveals its links with the Creator and all other creations.

The unity of life is a recurring theme in Indian Art.

Let it also be mentioned for the benefit of western critics that the Indian sculptors could not have created their masterpieces unless they had drawn their models from real life around them. They might have resorted to abstraction and idealisation, but like all artists anywhere in the world, their artistic creation is the result of first hand experience.

The rich Indian mythology, which is replete with stories of faith and devotion, aided the Indian sculptor in bringing out masterpieces depicting immortal legends like the '*Slaying of the demon Mahisha*', '*The rescue of the earth by Varaha*', '*The churning of the ocean*', and '*The descent of the Ganga*'.*

Yes, Indian art is rooted in tradition. Creativity is linked to cultural integrity which arises out of traditional moorings. Any nation which ignores its tradition and cultural integrity cannot produce lasting art.

Indian art, which has survived invasion and vandalism, is a tribute to the vitality of Indian Civilisation, which continues vibrant and alive, while many of its sister civilisations have perished away.

V.S. Naipaul, the noted author, has referred to India as a "wounded civilisation". Yes, wounded, no doubt, by incoherent appreciation, inadequate understanding and unkind criticism. But the

*Sculptures in Mahabalipuram.

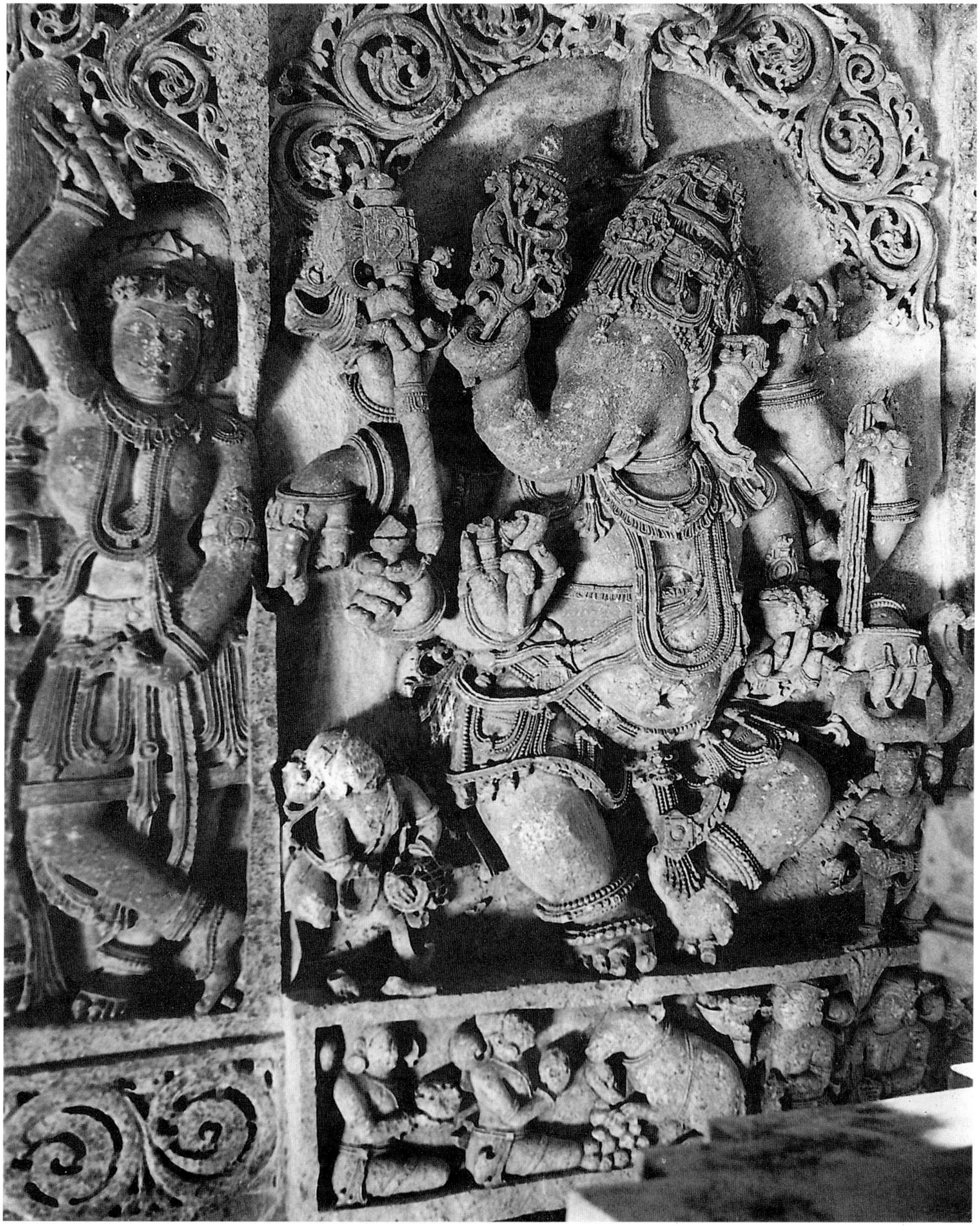

1. Dancing Ganesa, Hoysaleshwara temple, Halebid.

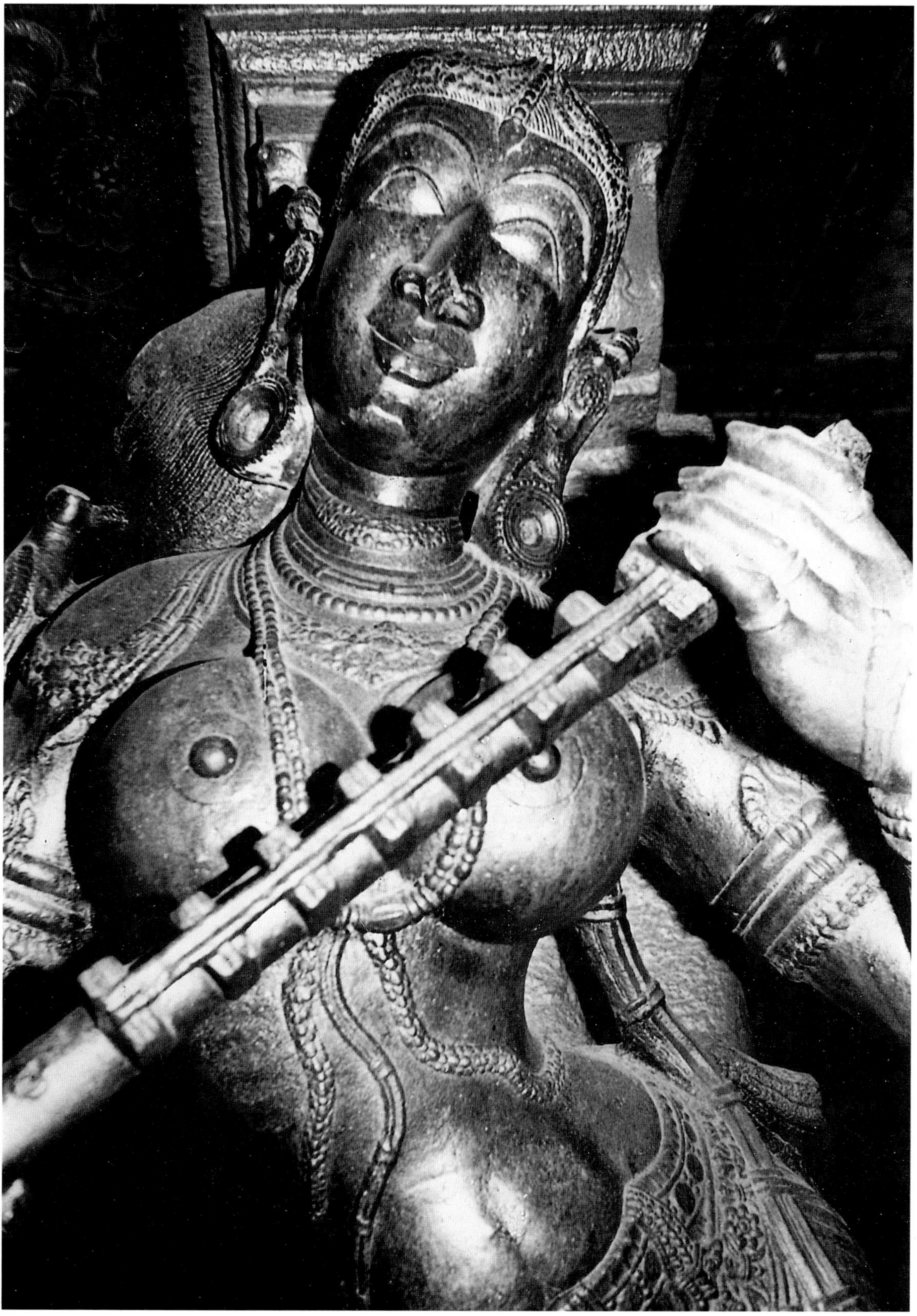

7B. A lute player, sculpture, Madurai temple.

wounds will heal. The sheen will return to the encrusted soul, if Indians realise the value of their heritage and its usefulness to the world.

Heinrich Zimmer, in his book *The Art of Indian Asia,* remarks, "Indian art, besides documenting the history of a majestic civilisation, opens a comparatively simple, delightful way into the timeless domain of the Indian spirit, for it renders in eloquent visual forms the whole message that India holds in keep for mankind."

India's message which Zimmer has referred to, which is the fountainhead of its artistic expression, is, to use Will Durant's own words:

"The tolerance and gentleness of the mature mind, the quiet content of the unacquisitive soul, the calm of the understanding spirit, and a unifying, pacifying love for all living things."

Periods and Places of Indian Art

Dates	*Period*	*Main Places*
3000-1500 B.C.	Indus Valley Civilisation	Mohenjodaro & Harappa (now in Pakistan)
321-184 B.C.	The Mauryan Period	Sarnath
185-72 B.C.	Sunga Dynasty	Sanchi, Bharhut, Bhaja, Bodhgaya
25 B.C.-300 A.D.	Andhra Dynasty	Amaravati
100-600 A.D.	Kushanas	Mathura
320-650 A.D.	The Guptas	Sarnath
600-850 A.D.	The Pallavas	Kanchipuram & Mamallapuram
550-750 A.D.	The Chalukyas	Aihole, Badami & Pattadakkal
750-975 A.D.	The Rashtrakutas	Elephanta & Ellora
730-1250 A.D.	Pala & Sena Dynasties	Nalanda
1076-1586 A.D.	Ganga Dynasty	Konarak
850-1150 A.D.	The Cholas	Thanjavur
1100-1310 A.D.	The Hoysalas	Halebid and Belur
950-1335 A.D.	The Chandellas	Khajuraho
1100-1350 A.D.	The Pandyas	Tiruvannamalai
1350-1565 A.D.	The Raya Dynasty	Vijayanagar (Hampi Ruins)
1560-1743 A.D.	The Nayaks	Madurai
1526-1857 A.D.	The Mughal Period	Delhi, Agra, Fatehpur Sikri

II

Sarnath

Where Buddha Preached his First Sermon

Sarnath, six miles north of Varanasi, is one of the four holy places connected with the Buddha. The other three are: *Lumbini*, where he was born, *Buddhagaya*, where he became enlightened, and *Kushinara* or *Kashia* (in Gorakhpur District), where he cast off his mortal coil. At *Sarnath* he preached his first sermon.

Sarnath is a distortion of the word *Sāranganatha*, which literally means "protector of deer". According to Cunningham, the place derives its name from the Siva temple by this name, located nearby. The epithet can apply to Buddha himself or a Bodhisattva incarnation. Sarnath was probably a deer-park.

It was at Sarnath that Buddha, after attaining enlightenment at Bodhgaya, propounded the famous four noble truths: *Ārya Satya Chatushtya.*

The *first* truth is that there is sorrow in the phenomenal world. The *second* relates to the origin and cause of sorrow.

The *third* explains the cessation of sorrow and the *fourth* expounds the eightfold path (*Arya Astangika Marga*).

The eightfold path comprises:

Right views,
Right aspirations,
Right speech,
Right conduct,
Right living,

Right effort,
Right mindfulness, and
Right meditation.

The first sermon of the Buddha, which he preached to his five disciples, Kondanna, Vappa, Bhaddiya, Mahanama and Assaji, is known as "*Dharmachakra Pravartana*" (Turning of the Wheel of Law).

Mahavagga clarified the master's teaching in the following eloquent words: "There are two extremes, O Monks, from which he who leads a religious life should abstain. What are those two extremes? One is a life of pleasure, devoted to desire and enjoyment, that is base, ignoble, unspiritual, unworthy, and unreal. The other life is a life of mortification. It is gloomy, unworthy, and unreal. The perfect one, O Monks, is removed from both the extremes and has discovered the way which lies between them: the *middle path* which enlightens the mind, which leads to rest, to knowledge, to enlightenment and to Nirvana."

The sanctity of Sarnath begins in the first sermon, but does not end there.

It was at Sarnath that the Buddha established the *Sangha* with 60 monks and sent them to various places to preach his Dharma.

Two hundred years after Buddha, came Asoka, the Mauryan emperor, a convert to Buddhism after the carnage at Kalinga and erected many monuments, the most famous of which was the monolithic pillar with the Lion Capital, adopted by India as the State Emblem and which stands majestically even today in the museum at Sarnath.

The Lion Capital with the four lions and the Dharmachakra is a magnificent example of Mauryan Art, a precious legacy which fully deserves the honour bestowed on it by the Republic of India.

The Sungas built a few stone railings at Sarnath *a la* Sanchi, during the first century B.C. while the Kushanas, the Great Mathura Builders, created a superb sandstone Bodhisattva.

But the golden age of Sarnath came under the Guptas, the most shining example of outstanding art being the seated Buddha image.

The image is a fine expression in stone of the meditative and compassionate Buddha giving the first message of deliverance to the world. The wheel or chakra, the symbol of the Dharma, occupies the centre of the pedestal and on its two sides are the figures of the five disciples to whom the first sermon was preached.

During Harsha's reign, Sarnath continued to flourish. Hiuen Tsang, the Chinese pilgrim, visited Sarnath and has left a vivid description of the monuments.

Sarnath's good fortune, which continued under the Pala kings, declined with Mahmud Ghazni's invasion in 1017.

Apart from the Lion Capital and the Guptan Buddha image, the other monuments of Sarnath deserving mention are: the Dhamek Stupa, the Dharmarajika Stupa, the main shrine and the monastery ruins.

The Dhamek Stupa was originally, probably, erected by Asoka, but the present ornamental covering belongs to the Gupta period.

The Dharmarajika Stupa was also built by Asoka, to enshrine the bodily relics of the Buddha.

A visit to Sarnath reminds us of three precious legacies that make all Indians proud:

Firstly, the *Heritage of the Buddha,* the compassionate one who preached:

"Let not one kill any living being
Let not one take what is not given to him
Let not one speak falsely
Let not one drink intoxicating drinks
Let not one be unchaste"

a message if carried out in action will alleviate all the sufferings in the world and produce the ideal man and the ideal society.

Secondly, *the glory of Asoka,* who woke up to realise the greatness of the Buddha's teaching and paid homage to the Master in the famous Lion Capital, which is one of the greatest masterpieces of plastic art of all times and has rightly become India's State Emblem, a composition of such astonishing perfection that Sir John Marshall ranked it "to anything of its kind in the ancient world" and which Will Durant described in these eloquent words: "We have four powerful lions, standing back to back on guard, and thoroughly Persian in form and countenance, but beneath is a frieze of well-carved figures including so Indian a favourite as the elephant, and so Indian a symbol as the Buddhist Wheel of the Law, and under the frieze is a great stone lotus, formerly mistaken for a Persian Bell Capital, but now accepted as the most ancient, universal and characteristic of all the symbols in Indian Art.

"Represented upright, with the petals turned down and the pistil or seed vessel showing, it stood for the womb of the world, or as one of the fairest of nature's manifestations, it served as the throne of God."

Thirdly, *the perfection in sculpture reached in the golden age of the Guptas,* symbolised by the magnificent seated Buddha image, preaching the sermon, a piece of sculpture in which the body sheds off all its toughness, attains full and soft soundness and exhales an aroma of complete ease and serenity. All this is achieved with the help of a soft and delicate modelling, a softly gliding, smoothly flowing, melting line and an utmost economy of plastic differentiation.

With these three nostalgic memories: of the Buddha and his teachings, of Asoka and Mauryan art, and of the golden age of the Guptas, we return from Sarnath with a spring in our steps, a lilt in our hearts and a tune on our lips, in homage to our heritage.

III

Sanchi

Sublimity in Stone

Known for its great Stupa, Sanchi lies 30 miles to the northwest of Bhopal, the capital of Madhya Pradesh and is approachable by road from the airport.

The story of Sanchi is one of Stupas, of the rise and fall of Buddhism, of the passing cavalcade of different dynasties and of transition from wood sculpture to stone sculpture.

A Stupa is basically a burial mound, hemispherical in shape, containing the remains of a dignitary. Eight Stupas containing the sacred relics of the Buddha are believed to have been built by Asoka, the great Mauryan Emperor at Sanchi. Among these the most important is Stupa One or the Great Stupa.

This Great Stupa is a massive structure, 54 feet in height and 120 feet in diameter, surrounded by a balustrade and surmounted by a stone umbrella—a symbol of royalty.

Though the nucleus of the existing monuments at Sanchi was laid by Asoka, it was really during the period of the Satavahana rulers (1st century B.C.) who overthrew the Sungas, that the four great balustrades around the main Stupa, containing glorious sculpture, were erected.

The Satavahanas were replaced by the Western Satraps (second century A.D.) who contributed very little to the monuments then existing at Sanchi.

During the Gupta rule (fourth century A.D.) a temple (temple no. 17) was constructed. King Harsha added some monasteries but after this last patron of Buddhism, Sanchi gradually faded into oblivion.

Apart from the three Stupas, the ruins at Sanchi comprise several temples and monasteries of artistic and historical interest.

The tall pillars—the extant ruins of temple no. 18—clearly betray Greek influence and are reminiscent of the Parthenon temple at Athens.

Temple no. 45 contains in its *sanctum sanctorum* an image of Buddha. It has also figures of Ganga and Yamuna carved at the base of its door-jambs.

The holocaust of successive invasions left Sanchi unaffected. So we have today the most glorious and ancient sculpture of the Satavahana period, nearly two thousand years old, looking fresh and intact.

The sculptors of Sanchi have dealt with stone as they would with wood, bamboo or ivory. The stone balustrade around the Stupas looks like a bamboo fence.

The sculpture on the four gateways is supposed to deal with incidents in Buddha's previous lives, as narrated in various *jataka* stories. But even without getting involved in the details of these stories, it is possible to enjoy these magnificent pieces of sculptural art, which depict elephants, horses, camels, lions, and men and women living their lives of work and love, amidst natural surroundings.

There are also *Yakshas* and *Yakshis*, carved out in exquisite beauty and placed in strategic positions.

In the pillars supporting their major gateways, there are also beautiful floral designs, in some of which, at least, one could discern clearly tantric motifs.

The Buddhist motifs like the **Dharma Chakra** or the Wheel of Law, the Lotus and the Lions, have no doubt been given pride of place in the architraves, but the sculptors of Sanchi have not ignored any aspect of life in their carvings. Scenes of war have been depicted with as much felicity as tender scenes of love.

Percy Brown remarks: "Few portals in any style of architecture can excel the array of rich symbolism and imagery which has been portrayed with such dramatic intensity on the Sanchi **Toranas**, the result entirely of Indian tradition and genius."

E.B. Havell, in his book *The Art Heritage of India*, observes:

"The Sanchi sculptures...are...magnificently decorative, and provide a most wonderful picture of Indian life and thought. The visits of the pilgrims to the sacred shrines, the stories told by camp fires, the fabled pre-existence of the Buddha in the form of bird and beast, and all the mysteries of untrodden primeval forests are revealed in a series of sculptures which, besides being most valuable for historical purposes, makes a most delightful, original Indian jungle-book.

"We can see, also, how strongly the idea of the essential unity of creation has taken hold of the Indian mind. For all nature is shown animated by a single purpose. Man and beast, gods and demi-gods, and the weird monsters of Indian mythology throng together to join in worship of the emblems of the Buddhist faith."

A description of the sculptures at Sanchi would be incomplete without a mention of the famous female bracket figure on the eastern gate of Stupa 1. The figure has been interpreted in diverse ways by art historians.

Some have referred to it as a **yakshi**, some as a treewoman as **vrikshaka**, some as **Aranyani** (of Vedic origin), some as **Salabhanjika**, and some as Dryad (wooden nymph of Greek mythology).

Havell considers this bracket figure "singularly fine in movement and skilfully modelled." He adds: "The style of it shows no trace of the Hellenic tradition, nor of the idealism of later Indian sculpture. It is a piece of simple forceful realism of Indian sculptors, before any attempt is made to idealise the human form. Nevertheless it would be difficult to find among the Gandharan sculptures anything to surpass it either in technique or artistic feeling."

H. Zimmer's views are more interesting. He says: "On the east gate at Sanchi hangs the Dryad (Vrikshaka), exhibiting the features that India has always cherished in the female...a vigorous dynamism pervades the form, the body swells with a living force...the limbs have been welded into a unity suffused by a gentle yet powerful circulation that visibly throbs in every part...this tree nymph has a perpetual pulsing, as though she personified the gently raging life-sap within the tree, which rises along the stem and expands into a crown to which she holds. She is full-blooded, and yet has the musical grace of a nimble dancing girl."

The presence of sensuous sculptures in temples and monuments built in honour of saintly personages is an intriguing phenomenon to foreigners and they try to bring in farfetched explanations to justify it. For example, on the so-called **Yakshis*** of Sanchi Michael Edwardes says: "In their frankly erotic poses they represent the world of illusion which the worshipper leaves behind as he enters the sacred enclosure. They also illustrate the use of sensual metaphor for spiritual purposes which is one of the unique features of Indian religious art."

One should not deny erudite foreigners the benefit of their preferences based on their observations and study. But the truth is *that the Indian sculptor has no inhibitions about celebrating the world of senses.* Like all true artists of all times, he has felt attracted by the beauty and grace of the human form, especially the female form, and given artistic expression to it, in myriad variations, with all the mastery and skill at his command.

In Sanchi, the sculptor has glorified all creation, not merely human beings. In fact, depiction of animal life predominates over that of human forms. The Sanchi sculpture represents the first memorable landmark of Indian art, when the true Indian genius, shorn of foreign influences, asserted itself, and gave full and free expression to its artistic feeling.

The overall feeling one gets after a visit to Sanchi (apart from pride in India's artistic heritage) is one of security and sublimity. The unseen, unrepresented presence of the Buddha pervades the whole atmosphere and reminds one of his eternal message of love, truth and peace.

---

*Yakshas and Yakshis are semi-celestial beings in Indian Mythology.

IV

Kanchipuram

The Golden Girdle of Goddess Kamakshi

Kanchipuram is situated 75 kms (47 miles) south of Chennai. Its anglicised version, **Conjeevaram**, still sticks to the beautiful silk sarees turned out by the handloom weavers of the place, which have become the rage of the fashionable elite the world over.

It is perhaps ironical that the fame of Kanchipuram today mainly rests on its silk sarees, but let it be stated for record that Kanchipuram is also the Golden City of a thousand temples and among the seven sacred cities of India.

The others are Ayodhya, Mathura, Hardwar, Kashi, Ujjain and Dwaraka.

Traditionally the seat of Kamakshi, Kanchi had been the capital of several successive empires, including the Pallavas, the Cholas, the Rayas of Vijayanagar which once flourished and fell. It was also a city of learning to Hindus, Buddhists and Jains and above all, a city sacred to both Vishnu and Siva.

Why the name Kanchipuram? There are many versions. Some believe it to have been derived from the name of a tree, but the most accepted of all explanations is that the name was derived from the Sanskrit word, *Kānchana,* for gold. Thus, **Kanchi** is a golden girdle worn by ladies of ancient India. Some scholars consider Kanchi 'as a girdle to earth'. All we may satisfy ourselves is that the term Kanchi is related to the gold in the city, in its heyday of prosperity. Kanchipuram thus remains the Golden City.

Though there are legendary and literary references to Kanchi from the Mauryan age to the end of the Sangam period in the third century A.D., Kanchi shot into prominence mainly as the capital of the Pallavas. During the sixth and seventh centuries A.D., when Mahendra Varman and Narasimha Varman (Mamalla), the great Pallava rulers, were in supremacy, some of the best temples were built in Kanchi.

Hiuen Tsang, the famous Chinese traveller, visited Kanchi in 646 A.D. and wrote: "The capital of the country is called Kanchipura. The soil is fertile and well cultivated and it produces abundant grains. There are also many flowers and fruits grown. It has precious gems and other articles. The climate is hot, people are courageous, binding themselves to the principle of honesty and truth. They highly esteem learning. There are some hundreds of **Sangharamas** and ten thousand priests. There are some 80 deva temples and many heretics called **Nirgranthas**..."

As a consequence of Narasimha Varman's siege of Vatapi (modern Badami) the Chalukyan rulers frequently attacked Kanchi and at least once it came under the Chalukyas. The Chalukyan ruler Vikramaditya II, being a connoisseur of art, wanted to recreate the temples of Kanchi in his territory. Accordingly, he took away the Kanchi sculptors and architects and created the Virupaksha temple on the banks of Malaprabha river (modern Pattadakkal).

After the Chalukyas came the Rashtrakutas, and then the great Cholas. Rajaraja made Kanchi the base for his military activities for his conquest towards the North.

Rajendra, Rajaraja's son and successor, reinforced the educational and religious institutions at Kanchi.

The Hoysalas and Pandyas also exercised some control over Kanchi during the 13th century. The Muslim invasion swept away all ruling dynasties from the Northern Deccan to Kanyakumari and the whole of the peninsula came under Muslim rule. Kanchi also met with the same fate, till it came under Vijayanagar Empire in 1336 A.D. and regained its prominence under the patronage of the Raya rulers. During this period, a distinct Dravidian style of art and architecture developed. The architectural splendour of the **Ekambaranatha** and **Varadaraja** temples are some of its standing examples.

Literature also received royal patronage from rulers like Krishnadevaraya, Achyuta and Sadasiva and literary output in

Sanskrit, Telugu, Kannada and Tamil reached the zenith during their rule. Religious thinkers like Vedantadesika, Vyasarayatirtha, Appayya Dikshitar and Tatacharya came on the scene.

Soon after the decline of the Vijayanagar empire, the city passed into the hands of Marathas and then to Aurangzeb in quick succession. The French who had heard of the fabulous wealth of the temples attacked and annexed Kanchi in 1760 A.D. Later, it came under British rule.

What a succession of rulers has the Golden City come under, and yet, despite political vicissitudes, its dominance in the fields of culture, religion and education has remained undiminished.

As C.R. Srinivasan observes in his book, *Kanchipuram Through the Ages* (Publishers: Motilal Banarsidass, Delhi), "The quest for knowledge drove **Manimekalai** of the Sangam age to this great city of learning; lured by the clarion call of this city, Mayurasarman of Banavasi enlisted himself as one of the aspirants in the city's advanced centre of vedic learning; the lofty ideals of Buddhism brought Hieun Tsang all the way from China.

"The growth and development of various religions such as Buddhism, Jainism, Saivism and Vaishnavism helped the city to carve a covetable niche in the annals of South Indian history. The sedulous patronage given to these religions which diffused and blended in the city in various periods and phases of history of Kanchi finds expression in the everlasting monuments that are in and around it..."

Though originally there were one thousand temples, today only 124 shrines remain. The earliest temple built is the **Kailasanatha** temple, dedicated to Siva; next is the **Vaikuntanatha Perumal** temple built by the Pallava Emperor Nandivarman II. Sculptures here depict the wars between Pallavas and Chalukyas.

Kanchi houses one of the five temples in honour of Lord Siva, representing five eternal elements (*Pancha Bhutam*). The Ekambareswara temple is symbolic of Earth. The others are: the Jambukeswara temple, near Tiruchirapalli, symbolic of Water, Tiruvannamalai, Fire, Kalahasti, Wind and Chidambaram, Ether.

The height of the entrance gopuram of the Ekambaranatha Swamy temple is 188 feet.

The Varadaraja Swamy temple has a hall of ninety-six pillars decorated with beautiful sculptures.

The significance of Kanchi is heightened by the fact that it is the seat of Kamakshi, the Goddess with beautiful eyes, whose temple has an association with Adi Sankara. The temple is one of the great trinity of temples, enshrining the Divine Mother, the other two being the Meenakshi temple of Madurai and the Visalakshi temple of Varanasi.

Great sages and poets have poured out their devotion to **Kanchi Kamakshi** in soulful poetry. Apart from Adi Sankara, we may list Durvasa (who wrote the **Saktimahimna Stotra**) and the great **Mookakavi**, who has written the immortal **Mooka Panchasati**, a poem of 500 verses, full of surrender, which was often referred to by the venerable sage of Kanchi in his discourses.

The best way to end this homage to Kanchi is to quote a verse from **Mookapanchasati**:

"We do not sport with riches; we do not serve evil men; we do not indulge in pleasures; we are not afraid of the fear of samsara; we ever meditate in our minds on the tender shoot-like feet of the Spouse of Siva, the Destroyer of Cupid, who is fond of Kanchi."

V

Mamallapuram (Mahabalipuram)

Monumental Monoliths of Mamalla

Havell, noted author of that famous book, *The Ideals of Indian Art* (published in 1920), discerns qualities of deep serenity and austerity in Indian art in general and in the sculptural remains at Mamallapuram, in particular.

Mamallapuram, currently known as Mahabalipuram, is a coastal town facing the Bay of Bengal, 30 miles south of Madras (now Chennai) the capital of Tamil Nadu.

It was a thriving seaport, during the heyday of Pallava rule and it was from here that Indian emigration to South East Asia took place.

The creator of this port was the renowned Pallava ruler, Narasimhavarman I, who was known as Mamalla (literally meaning Great Fighter). Mamalla ruled from about 630 A.D. to 668 A.D.

We do not know how Mamallapuram looked during the seventh and eighth centuries, but today the sculptural feast that greets the visitor includes monolithic monuments called *Rathās*, ten cave halls called *Mandapas*, a few rock-cut bas reliefs, the largest in the world, and a "Shore Temple", the only survivor of seven such believed to have been built on the salty shore, susceptible to sea erosion.

The Pallava style of architecture and sculpture as seen in Mamallapuram is significant in two ways: one, it is a blend of Hindu and Buddhist styles, and two, it is the mother of sculptural masterpieces in Cambodia and Java.

But what impresses the visitor to Mamallapuram is not the special style developed by the Pallava craftsmen but the tremendous dramatic content imported into the sculpture by the sculptors. The puranic stories depicted in the various Mandapas and in the bas reliefs are unparalleled in the grandiose design, remarkable attention to detail and perfect finesse in execution.

The most outstanding dramatic presentation in sculpture is the Mahishasura Mardini panel. The figure of Durga against the buffalo demon, Mahishasura, is depicted in such a beautiful manner that one feels the entire movement of war, though the figures themselves are not grotesque.

As Michael Edwardes observes in his book, *Indian Temples and Palaces,* "the scene, though it tells a story of almost brutal drama, is as gentle and restrained as all Pallava sculpture. Yet there is no loss of vigour, and the figures of the Goddess seated on the lion and the surrounding gods sweep irresistibly forward."

One has seen the depiction of Mahishasura Mardini in Ellora and Halebid, but the masterpiece in Mamallapuram is unique in its beauty.

The other sculptural panels worth mentioning are the *Anantasayana,* Vishnu reclining on the serpent; *Adivaraha,* the incarnation of Vishnu as the boar to rescue mother earth from the surging waters; *Trivikrama,* Vishnu measuring the universe in three steps; *Govardhana Krishna,* the beloved of the cowherds who protects them from the wrath of Indra by lifting the mountain; and *Gajalakshmi,* a depiction of the daughter of the ocean being bathed by elephants.

"*Descent of the Ganges*" is the theme depicted in the giant bas relief. Sometimes the legend depicted is mistaken for Arjuna's penance, but the details shown indicate definitely that the story is that of the descent of Ganga to earth. It is a story worth recapitulating:

Sagara, a renowned ruler of the Ikshvaku dynasty, wanted to perform the *Asvamedha* sacrifice to establish his suzerainty. Accordingly, a horse with auspicious marks was let loose, accompanied by Sagara's sons and a well equipped army. Indra, afraid of a threat to his own sovereignty, stole the horse and left it in the hermitage of Kapila. Sagara's sons tried to attack Kapila but were reduced to ashes by him. Sagara's grandson, *Ansuman*, approached Kapila and was told that the dead could be revived by bringing the heavenly Ganga to earth.

Accordingly, Ansuman tried, but could not succeed. His son Dilipa also met with no success.

Ultimately, Dilipa's son, Bhagiratha, after severe penance, got the blessings of Brahma that Ganga would descend to the earth, but subject to the condition that the impact of her descent to the earth should be broken lest the earth got washed away.

Bhagiratha prayed to Lord Siva. The Lord pleased by his penance received the turbulent Ganga in His matted locks and only then let her flow gently over the ashes of Sagara's sons, who immediately came back to life.

The representation of the above myth in Mamallapuram is quite different from the one at Elephanta. Here as Michael Edwardes writes: "The episodes converge from left and right on the central cleft in which the river flows to earth. There a giant serpent floats up the torrent, his face set in rapt devotion as is that of the serpent queen who follows him. There are other deities of the water, and on either side crowd all the living things of the world who have come to watch the saving of their World. Bhagiratha is shown twice doing penance (once before Brahma and again before Siva). The sculptural treatment is calm, there are no mysteries or horrors, no dramatics or violent effects, only serenity and repose. Even the animals seem quiet and lost in bliss."

The Rathas of Mamallapuram monolithic shrines, named in honour of the five Pandava heroes, have maximum Buddhist influence in their architecture. Learned scholars have done painstaking research on their architectural and iconographic survey and written volumes. In fact, there is a single book on the Dharmaraja Ratha alone, *Dharmaraja Ratha and its Sculptures* by K.R. Srinivasan (Publishers: Abhinav Publications, New Delhi).

The shore temple which stands aloof and alone is a structural innovation of the early eighth century A.D. The rows of Nandi, the bull around the temple, add a peculiar charm to the shore temple.

A description of the sculptural marvels of Mamallapuram would be incomplete without a mention of the treatment of animals by the Pallava sculptors.

The elephant is the most prominent among the animals depicted. There is a life-size elephant separately carved out, apart from the gigantic ones on the rock-cut bas relief.

Lions have been shown as also deer, monkeys, cats and serpents.

Will Durant considers the lovely stone deer of Mamallapuram as one of the masterpieces of Indian sculpture.

A friend of mine, a resident of Madras, was once invited by me to accompany me on a visit to Mahabalipuram. He asked cynically: "What is there to see at Mahabalipuram—a few rocks?" His reaction reminded me of the adage: "Nearest to the Church, farthest from God."

The great sculptural masterpieces bequeathed to us by our illustrious ancestors are very much around us, in close proximity. It would be a crime if we ignore them or fail to appreciate their artistic value.

Mamallapuram is one such precious legacy, for which we should bow in reverence to the Pallava rulers who so generously patronised the talented Pallava sculptors and architects and enabled the creation of such mammoth, monolithic marvels, which are the cynosure of our pride and the envy of the world.

VI

Temples of Chamba

Himachal Pradesh abounds in places of great scenic beauty and several magnificent temples, important from the point of view of art, architecture, history and religious philosophy. Despite the publicity given by the tourist departments, many outside the state are not aware of the magnificent treasures which lie nestled in the beautiful interior regions, lying at the foothills of Himalayas.

Severe climatic conditions, lack of easy communication facilities and the inaccessibility of many of the higher regions are all responsible for preventing a larger number of visitors from discovering the precious legacies bequeathed by our ancestors in Himachal Pradesh.

A visit to Chamba is rewarding from many points of view. One can admire the majesty and grandeur of the Himalayas, one can be awestruck by the torrential fury and speeding current of the river Ravi—the main river of the Chamba district—one can enjoy the panoramic beauty of the Chamba valley, and the simplicity and charm of the people, skilled in art and craft, especially the art of embroidery. But all this is nothing compared to the thrill one gets when one confronts the temples of Chamba.

Everyone knows the famous places of pilgrimage in Himachal Pradesh: the temple of Vajreshwari Devi in Kangra, the famous temple of Jwala Mukhi, 34 kilometres from Kangra, the temple of Chintpurni, Baijnath, Chamunda Devi, Naina Devi, Paonta Sahib. But to me, the temples of Chamba (including those of Brahmour) represent something valuable from the point of view of art, history and religion.

Before I proceed to describe what is in store in these temples for the curious visitor, let me mention some mundane details as to how one, coming from outside, can reach Chamba and savour its mysterious delicacies.

The best way to come to Chamba is from Pathankot, a place connected by air and rail. If one takes the Jammu Tawi Express from Delhi, one reaches at six or so in the morning. From Pathankot, Chamba is about three hours drive by road. One can take a bus, taxi or jeep. Considering the conditions of the roads in the interior and if one has also to visit Brahmour, the best mode of conveyance is a jeep or a trekker.

The road drive from Pathankot to Chamba is highly enjoyable for one main reason. Apart from the beauty of the Himalayas, one becomes acquainted with the grandeur of the river Ravi.

Since Ravi is a very important river in the context of the Chamba District, I would like to mention a few interesting facts about this great river, one of the five great rivers of western India. The name Ravi is a distortion of the word *Iravati*, mentioned in ancient Sanskrit literature, which is considered by some to be the same as *Parusni*, a river mentioned in the *Rig Veda*. Even today, in the upper regions, the river is called *Rauti* or *Irauti*. It is interesting to know that Alexander's historians called it *Hydraotes* or *Rhouadis*, both derived from the name *Iravati*. The total length of the river is 450 miles, of which 75 to 80 miles are in Chamba District. The Chamba town is located on the banks of the Ravi.

Now a little about the history of Chamba. Though claims are made about the early colonisation of western Himalayas in the Vedic period, the foundation of the state of Chamba (or Champa) appears to have taken place in the middle of the sixth century A.D., the original capital being *Brahmapura*, which is the present Brahmour.

The main temples, the remnants of which are still seen, were constructed in the seventh century A.D., during the reign of Meru Varman, who was the eighth Raja in succession from Meru, the Founder.

The most important of these temples are: Manimahesh, Lakshana Devi, Ganesha and Narsingh. The place where the temples are located is known as *Churasi* which literally means 84. When one first hears of the *Churasi* temples, one expects to see 84 temples, but sees only four. The tradition is that 84 sages visited Sahil Varma, one of the Rajas, and pleased with the Raja's hospitality, blessed him with progeny and prosperity. The place hallowed by the visit of the 84 sages took the name of *Churasi* and is held in veneration by the people.

Sahil Varma had a daughter by the name of *Champavati*, from whom the name of the state Chamba has probably evolved. This is confirmed by the fact that Sahil Varma ruled in the early tenth century and shifted the capital from Brahmour to Chamba near about 920 A.D.

Any visitor to the temples of Brahmour should not miss four brass images: the image of Lakshana Devi, Ganesha and Narasimha as also the Bull in front of Mani Mahesh temple. These images, exquisite in conception and execution, are in the late Guptan style and represent a high watermark of Indian metal architecture.

In the image of Lakshana Devi, the Goddess is conceived as *Mahishasuramardini*, Durga who destroys Mahisha, the Buffalo-monster. She rests Her right foot on the head of the killed Buffalo Demon, after having driven Her trident into his neck, while with Her left hand She catches the demon's tail and lifts his whole body up, almost vertically. In anatomical treatment, hair style, ornaments and costumes, Guptan influence is clearly seen. The Goddess is depicted as four armed, the other two arms holding a sword and a bell respectively.

The theme of *Mahishasuramardini*—a theme extolled in *Markandeya Purana* in *Devi Mahatmya* or *Saptasati*—has been dealt with by the Pallavas in Mahabalipuram, the Chalukyas in Badami caves and the Guptas in Bhumara, as also in the Udayagiri caves.

But the impact of the unique conception so beautifully executed in the temple of Lakshana Devi is awe-inspiring and sends cold shivers in the pious visitor, when he sees the image for the first time.

The images of Ganesha and Narasimha are also unique in their beauty. The four-armed Ganesha holds the broken tusk in one hand, fruits in another, an axe in the third.

Muscles of the abdomen are shown prominently. Also beautifully depicted are the crescent moon, the crown and the symmetrically shaped ears.

The image of *Narasimha*, the half-man half-lion incarnation of Vishnu who destroyed the demon *Hiranyakasipu* for the sake of His devotee, Prahlada, reminds one of the Kathakali characters of Kerala.

One has seen gigantic bull (Nandikeswara) images in the Chola temple in Tanjore, in Mysore and at several other places but none can match the elegance of this brass bull in Mani Mahesh temple, diminutive, decorative and exuding devotion to the Lord.

An outstanding feature of the Lakshana Devi temple is the fine wood carving in front of the *Sanctum Sanctorum*, the intricately carved figures which are reminiscent of Kashmir and Gandhara styles. Despite the ravages wrought by 13 centuries, some of the wood carvings are still intact, thanks to highly resistant quality of the deodar wood. Thus one can still see and enjoy the Mithuna figures half-man half-bird and half-woman half-bird, winged lions, deities, kneeling Yakshas and a gamut of floral decoration in exquisitely carved pillars.

In Chamba town itself there are ten temples, five dedicated to Vishnu, three to Siva and two to the Devi.

Of these, six are located on the bank of the Ravi river—three Vaishnavite temples and three Saivite.

In architecture, these temples fall under the category of *Shikhara* temple, like the ones one finds in Bhubaneshwar and elsewhere in the plains. There is, however, an important difference in the Chamba temples: an umbrella-shaped covering of wood or zinc is placed over and around the *Amalaka* stone placed on the spire, which reminds one of the pinnacles of most Kerala temples, the practical necessity being to protect the temples from heavy snowfall and rain.

The temples of Chamba, on the banks of Ravi, roughly belong to the tenth century. The most important one is the Lakshminarayan temple, with its image of white marble, and the other is that of Gauri Shankar, with its beautiful brass image of Siva and Parvati, along with their vehicle, the Bull.

On the outside walls of some of these temples, there are tiny, beautiful sculptures depicting the childhood sports of the cowherd deity, Krishna, who plays the flute.

The two other Vishnu temples in Chamba town are the Hari Rai and Bansi Gopal temples, the former fully decorated with carvings.

Of the two Devi temples, the temple of Vajreshwari or Bhagavati outside the town has fine sculpture. The temple of Champavati in the town is the oldest temple. It has a fine brass image in the *Sanctum Sanctorum* and a pair of stone lions (one grown up and the other a cub) in the frontyard.

While one is proud of the precious legacy bequeathed by our ancestors in the temples of Chamba—a legacy sheltered from the ravages of foreign invaders, thanks to the snowclad mountain barriers, one wishes that these ancient temples could be preserved with greater care and attention by the present and succeeding generations.

What remains in the form of ruins is only a small part of the glory that was—I am sure that painstaking archaeological pursuits will definitely unearth many more treasures, hidden underground, indicative of the great civilisation that once flourished in this pretty, happy valley, in the cradle of the Himalayas.

As one returns from a visit to the temples of Chamba, travelling along the road that runs side by side with the forceful river, Iravati, getting glimpses of the majesty and grandeur of the Himalayas, certain images stand out in the memory and kindle one's pride in the past, which is our history, our art, our culture and civilisation.

What are those images? The majestic silhouettes of the six Shikhara temples standing on the banks of Ravi? The ruins of the Churasi temples in Brahmour calling to one's mind vivid pictures of learned sages visiting a flourishing Ruler, sounds of Vedic chants and the smouldering fires of the sacrificial rites, tingling of temple bells announcing the evening worship in the Mani Mahesh temple? The stance of the metallic Nandi Bull standing in devotion before the Lord? The captivating charm of Lakshana Devi, destroying the Buffalo Demon, with an enviable ease, or the fascinating brass images of Ganesha, the Darling Deity and Narasimha, the protector of Prahlada? The majesty and grandeur of Lakshminarayan or the beauty of the Divine Couple, Gauri Shankar, carved in imperishable metal, the realistic icons of the roaring lions in front of the Champa Devi temple? Or the marvellous wood carvings of the angelic couples and floral designs in the frames and pillars of the Lakshana Devi temple in Brahmour?

I cannot defintely say. But this much I know: the haunting memories of what I have seen in Chamba temples thrill me and fill me with a gladness and aesthetic satisfaction, rarely equalled on other occasions. This is an experience which I would wish everyone to share, by making a visit to the temples of Chamba.

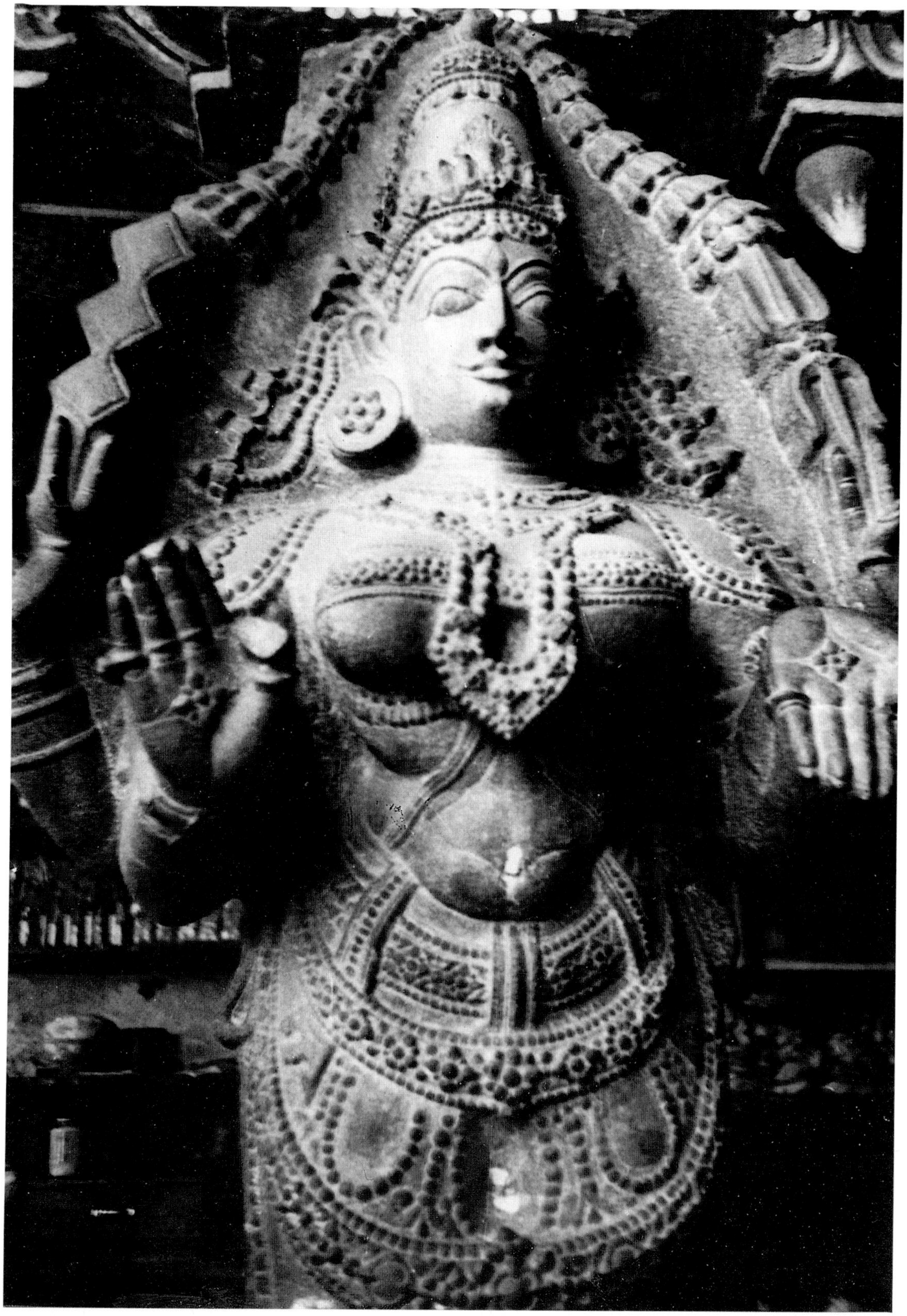

7C. One of the eight Saktis, sculpture, Madurai temple.

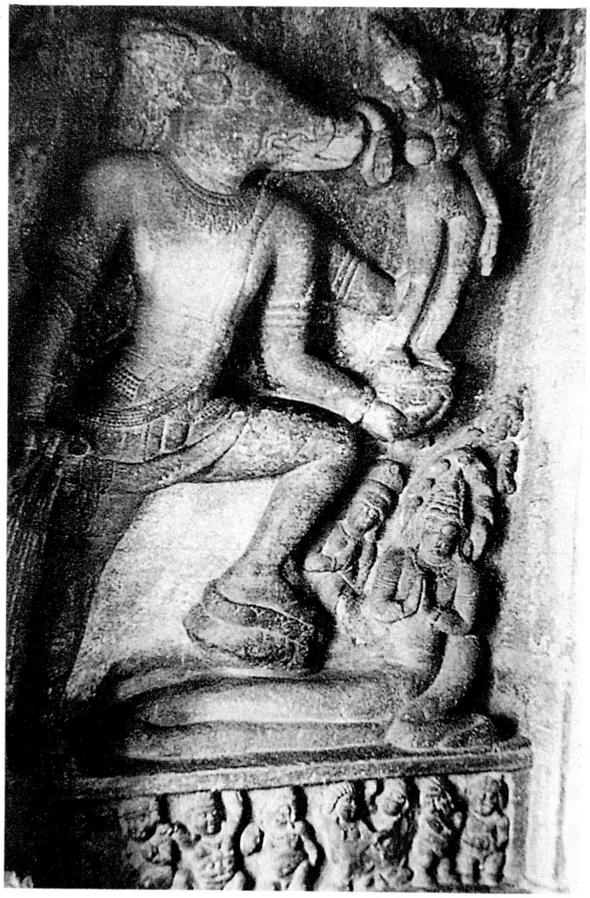

16. Varaha, Badami cave 3.

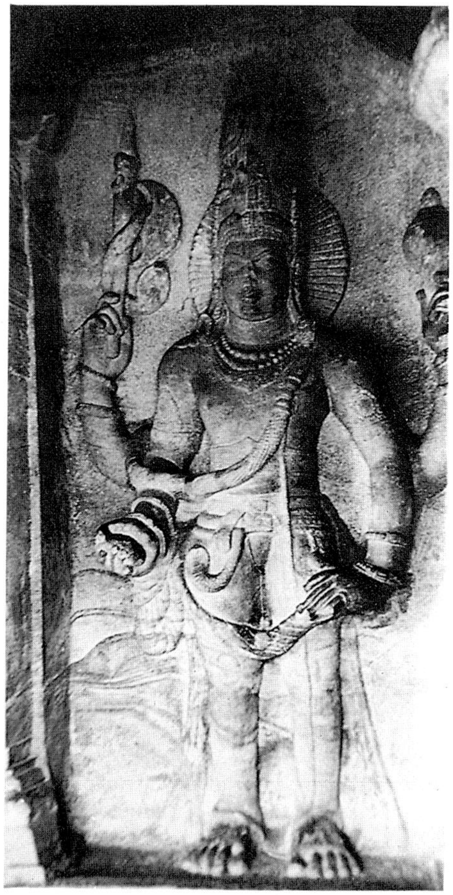

16A. Vishnu, Badami.

17. Mandu Jal Mahal.

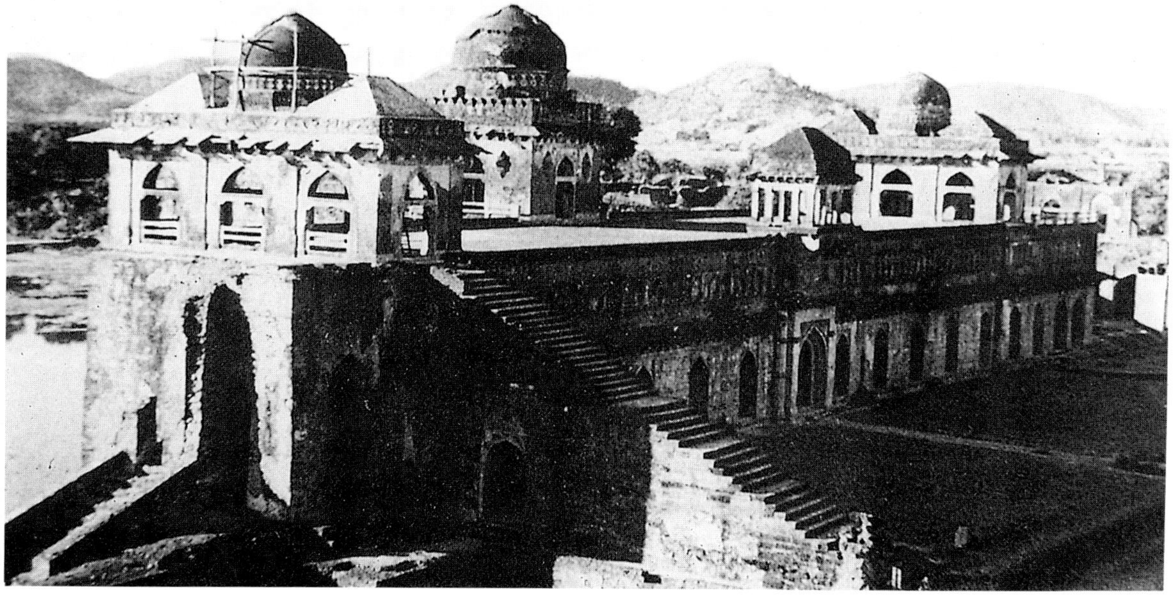

VII

Aihole

The Artless Art of the Chalukyas

Between the sixth and sixteenth centuries, a number of powerful dynasties ruled India south of the Vindhyas and left their cultural impress in valuable monuments which survive till today making us proud of our heritage.

Of these, the earliest were the Chalukyas who ruled between 550 A.D. and 750 A.D., the others being the Rashtrakutas (750-975 A.D.), the Pallavas (600-850 A.D.), the Cholas (850-1150 A.D.), the Hoysalas (1100 to 1310 A.D.), the Pandyas (1100 to 1350 A.D.) and the Nayaks (1560 to 1743 A.D.).

The territories controlled by these dynasties were comparatively small, but the artistic legacies they left behind are limitless in value.

We owe Ellora and the Elephanta to the Rashtrakutas, Mamallapuram and Kanchipuram to the Pallavas, Thanjavur to the Cholas, Belur and Halebid to the Hoysalas, Chidambaram and Tiruvannamalai to the Pandyas, and Madurai to the Nayaks.

The legacy of the Chalukyas can be seen in Aihole, Badami and Pattadakkal. All the three places lie within a short distance of each other (10 to 15 miles). They are approachable by road from Hubli—a distance of 80 miles.

While visiting Badami, we shall have a peep into the history of the Chalukyas, whose founder member was the great Pulikesin

I, the sworn enemy of the Pallavas of Kanchi. Though Badami was the capital of the Chalukyas, the Aihole monuments belong to a period earlier than that of the Badami sculptures.

William Willets considers Aihole to be the birthplace of the medieval temple.

The name Aihole possibly means the place of five rivers. *Ai* means five and *hole* means rivers in Kannada. There is also a view that the real name of the place is *Aiwalli.*

At first sight, one gets a mistaken impression that there is nothing much to see in Aihole. The only monument that stands out is the Durga temple. This was probably built during 600-642 A.D.

Zimmer's description of the Durga temple cannot be improved upon: "It comprises a porch, a main hall and an innermost sanctuary surmounted by a spire that is now in ruins. The pillared porch on the two sides scanning the length of the building widens to a gallery that encircles the structure meant for the ritual circumbulation."

Among the notable sculptures of the Durga temple are the *Mahishasuramardini, Varaha, Vishnu* and *Siva* icons which have been repeated with greater finesse at Badami and later at Mamallapuram.

The other monuments worth noting at Aihole are *Huchaparva Matha* which contains lovely Maithuna couples, the *Mallikarjuna Temple* whose sanctum sanctorum has a beautiful entrance carved ornamentally, the temple adjoining the Konti-Godi which has ceiling sculpture depicting the trinity: Brahma, Vishnu and Siva, the like of which does not exist in any other temple in India. The *Chakragudi Temple* and the *Ravanaphadi Cave* also contain exquisite sculpture pieces.

Zimmer's observations on the sculptures at Aihole are worth quoting: "This early Chalukya sculpture is—if possible—superior even to the Gupta. The weight and the matter on the stone has vanished, obliterated by the perfectly natural playful contortions of the floating bodies, and the patterns of the flying couples have been projected with a fluent skill that has rendered forms derived not from the world of waking consciousness but from vision vigorously carved in the round, the chisel providing for deep and powerful shadows, the apparitions, are yet immaterial and unearthly...in these forms, the quality of phantasmagoric substance has been masterfully imparted to a solid mass of gross and earthly stone.

"To forms hewn from solid stone there has been given unearthly intangibility and lightness of sheer vision, the matter of rock being transmuted into shapes of foam and mist comporting perfectly with the subtle mind substance of super-sensuous experience. *Indeed, I wonder whether in the artistic tradition of mankind, there exists another style in which this effect has been aspired to with such fervour and realised with consummate ease.* The works betray no trace of strain or exertion on the part of the artist craftsman."

So much for the eulogy on the Aihole sculpture. Now a little bit on William Willets' assertion that Aihole is the birthplace of the medieval Indian temple architecture.

A look at the Aihole temples, the Chakragudi temple and the Mallikarjuna temple, would indicate how the Aihole architects laid the foundations for the more elaborate temple spires at Mamallapuram, Thanjavur, Bhubaneshwar, Nagda and Khajuraho.

As Michael W. Meister writes, "The stone temple has grown out of a process of compaction and reduplication over the face of the Mass: first a decoration then as mass with this constant rhythm between compaction and reduplication has been the operating principle throughout the history of the Hindu temple, from region to region, style to style, period to period." The Aihole craftsmen have shown the path for others to follow.

A visit to Aihole is a pilgrimage in more senses than one. The pioneering efforts at temple building are no doubt impressive. The tributes paid in stone to man-woman love arrest the attention of western connoisseurs. The depiction of puranic legends like the destruction of *Mahishasura* and the *Vāmana Avatar** is awe inspiring. The beautiful ornamental door of the Sun Temple rivals the work of the jeweller on gold.

---

*Dwarf-incarnation of Vishnu.

VIII

Badami

The Bastion of Chalukyan Splendour

William Willets, the famous art critic, in an article written in the *Illustrated Weekly of India* of September 8, 1963, remarked: "Without the achievement of Badami, it is true to say, there would have been no subsequent triumph at Ellora or Mamallapuram. Selecting his themes mainly from the **Matsya**, **Harivamsa**, and other Vaishnava Puranas, the Badami sculptor seems to have translated them, then and there, into permanently satisfying plastic embodiments which were unhesitatingly adopted by later schools. If Aihole is the birthplace of the medieval temple, then Badami must surely be regarded as the foundry in which were cast the iconographic prototypes of medieval Saivite and Vaishnavite thematic sculpture."

These words of Willets had excited my imagination and created an incipient urge in me to see the caves of Badami but my visit could materialise only several years later in 1979.

Badami is on the Hubli-Sholapur railway line, but for those coming from Bombay or Bangalore, the best method is to get down at Hubli and travel a distance of 80 miles by road to Badami and get back to Hubli after visiting the caves.

Today Badami is only a taluka town, but once upon a time it was the flourishing capital of the great Chalukyas.

Who were the Chalukyas? The legends indicate that they were a Northern Kshatriya race, who emigrated from Rajasthan to Deccan region, sometime during the fifth century. The founder of the

Chalukya power was one Jayasimha who was followed by his son Rana Raja. The latter's successor was Pulikesin I, who ascended the throne about 543 A.D. and made **Vatapi** or Badami his capital.

Pulikesin's successor was Kirtivarman who ascended the throne in 567 A.D. and ruled for about a quarter of a century. When Kirtivarman died in 592 A.D., his younger brother, Mangalaraja, ascended the throne, overruling the claims of Kirtivarman's minor sons.

Mangalaraja (also known as Mangalesa) fought wars and expanded his territory. It was during his time that the most important cave temple (Cave III) was excavated at Badami.

Pulikesin II, the most prominent Chalukya ruler, came to power in 635 A.D. There was conflict between Chalukyas under him and the Pallavas led by Narasimhavarman I who ultimately stormed the Chalukyan capital in 642 A.D. and killed Pulikesin II.

With Pulikesin's death, Chalukyas ceased to be a dominant power, though his successors continued to rule and fight with the Pallavas.

The dynasty came to an end in 750 A.D., the last ruler being Kirtivarman III.

During the four centuries or so, when they wielded power, the Chalukyas patronised art and religion and built the imposing temples at Badami, Aihole and Pattadakkal.

There are four cave temples at Badami. Three are Hindu temples constructed between 550 A.D. and 580 A.D. and the fourth is a Jain temple built later in 650 A.D. All of them are marked by ingenuity and sculptural excellence.

The late Dr. Burgess wrote of the Badami caves as follows: "They stand as to arrangements of parts between Buddhist Viharas and the later Brahmanical examples at Ellora, Elephanta and Kanheri."

The sculpture retains the stylistic features of classical Guptan Art. Though contemporaneous with Vakataka school of Ajanta, it is much more vital.

Dr. S.K. Saraswati remarks that Ajanta sculpture suffers from "mental stupor and drowsy exhaustion", whereas at Badami, "the live rock bursts forth under the impress of a superhuman and aboriginal vitality."

In the first cave, on the left of the verandah, is a Dwarpal (door-keeper) with a Nandi over him. Opposite this Dwarpal is a figure of Siva, five feet high with 18 arms, dancing the Tandava.

In the main hall of this cave, we have Harihara with four hands and on the right Ardhanareeswara, attended by Nandi Bull and the skeleton Bhringi. There are also sculptures of *Mahishasura-mardini, Ganesha* and *Skanda* on the other walls.

In the second cave, we have the depiction of the *Varaha* avatar of *Vishnu,* and the *Trivikrama* panel.

The third cave is considered the finest of the lot. Eleven steps lead upto the cave. The facade has six pillars, the brackets of which contain fine mithuna figures of amorous couples and Siva and Parvati. Elaborate festoons have been carved on the columns of the pillars below which are medallions with groups of figures.

There is a statue of Narasimha, eleven feet high at the western end of the verandah. On the southern wall is *Harihara.* There are also depictions of *Vāmana* and *Varāha* avatars in this cave, as also of Vishnu seated on *Ananta,* the serpent.

The mythological legend, "*the churning of the ocean*", has also been carved out on the cross beams of the cave.

There are also lingering fragments of frescoes in Cave III indicating a link with the artists of Ajanta.

It is a remarkable feature of Cave III that though the sculptures mainly depict incarnations of Vishnu, the central object of worship is the *Siva-Linga.* The Chalukyas were well aware that the trinity—*Vishnu, Siva* and *Brahma*—are but the facets of the One Supreme.

In the fourth (Jain) cave, there is a seated statue of Mahavira.

In the book *Legacy of India* edited by G.T. Garrett, there is a chapter on Indian Art and Archaeology by K.DE.B. Codrington. In a delightful passage, discussing the carvings of couples on the pillars of cave three at Badami, Codrington writes: "In India, spirit and flesh are not antithetical...sensation and understanding, the delightful and the moral, image and imagination are not opposed, but one...In India, lovers decorate the temple...Of this class of Indian sculpture no more examples exist than the little couples of figures that adorn the Badami pillar capitals."

Commenting on Codrington's remarks, William Willets notes: "They (the figures) are not so very little, each pair being over three feet high, but they are certainly the most idyllic images of *Mithuna* ever conceived."

Zimmer sees in the female figures of Badami a "tender voluptuousness, approaching celestial sensuality."

Apart from the caves, at Badami there are also structural temples, like the *Malegetti Sivalaya*, "the temple of the Garland maker", located on the northern hill (built in early seventh century) and very simple in form.

An inscription in the third cave at Badami refers to it as a "shrine beyond the dreams of men and gods." After a visit to Badami, one tends to disagree with this inscription.

The Badami cave temples were conceived in the dreams of the Chalukyan rulers and converted into reality by craftsmen with painstaking skill, vitality and labour. It is hence untrue to say that these shrines were beyond the dreams of men.

As we leave the pinkish-brown sandstone rocks of Badami, glowing in the gorgeous rays of the setting sun, we salute the great Chalukyan rulers who caused these temples to be built and the great anonymous artists and craftsmen of India who built them with love, piety, and devotion, over 1400 years ago.

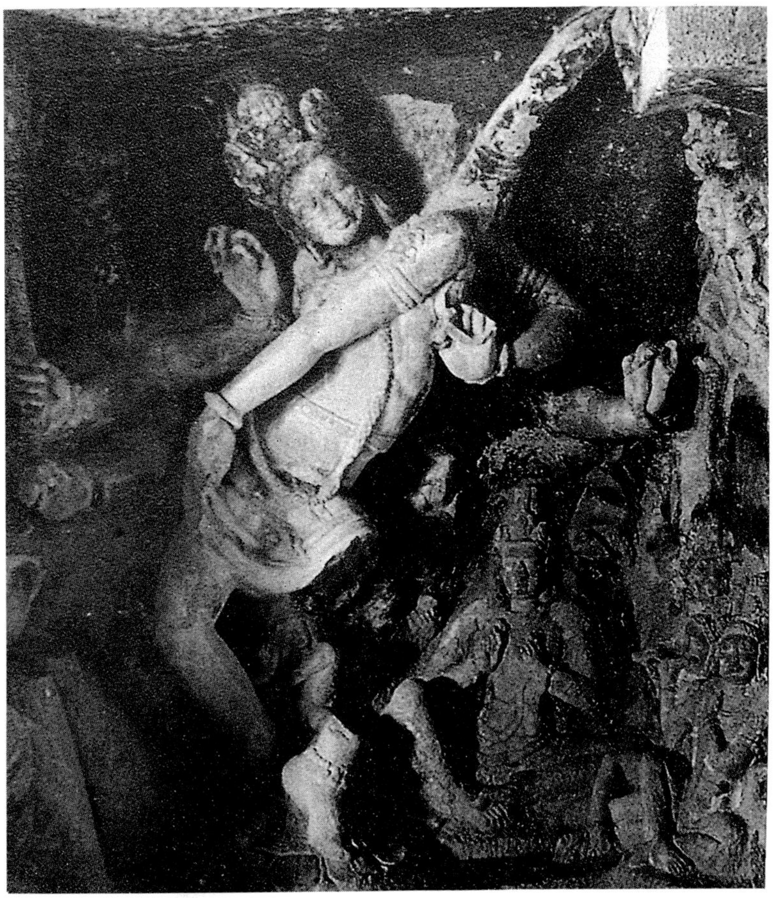

18. Nataraja, Ellora.

18A. Ravana lifting Kailasa, Ellora.

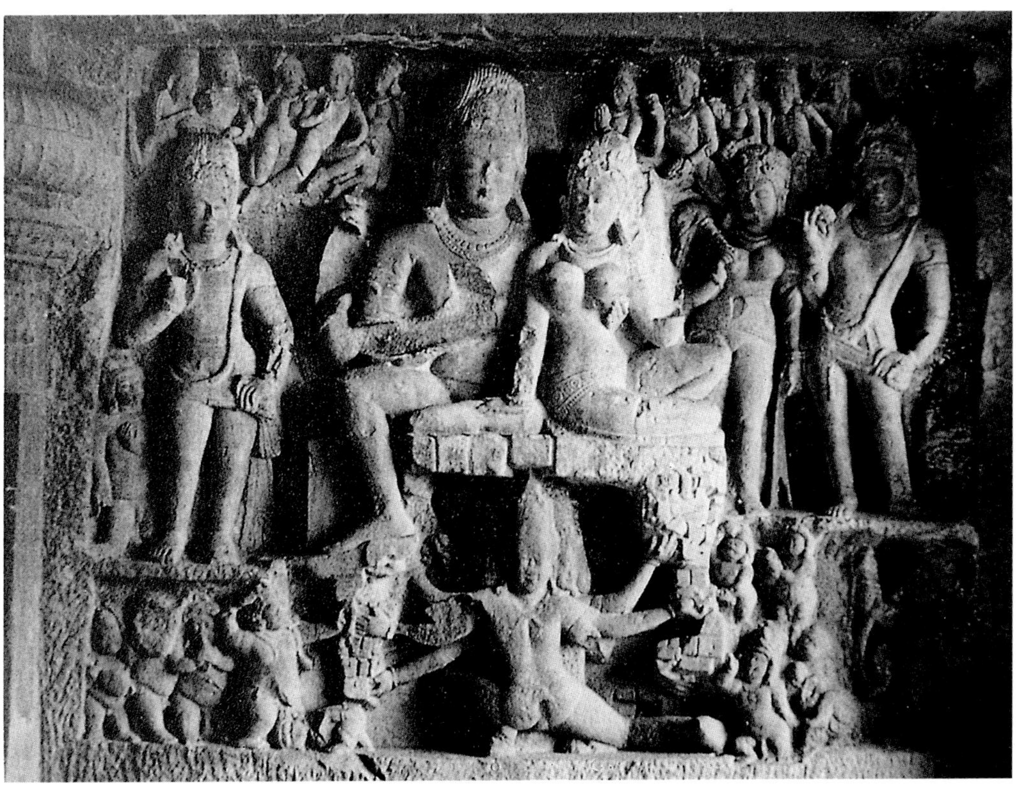

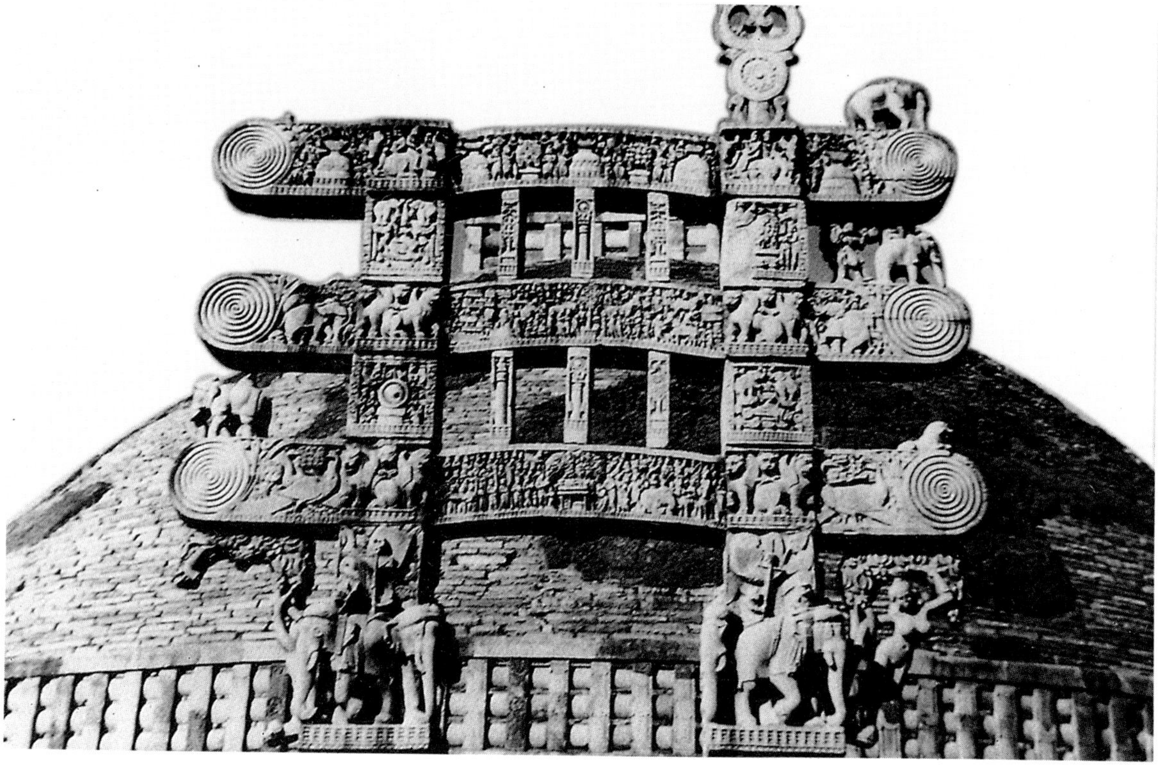

19. Sanchi East Gate, Main Stupa.

19A. Sanchi Ariputa Stupa.

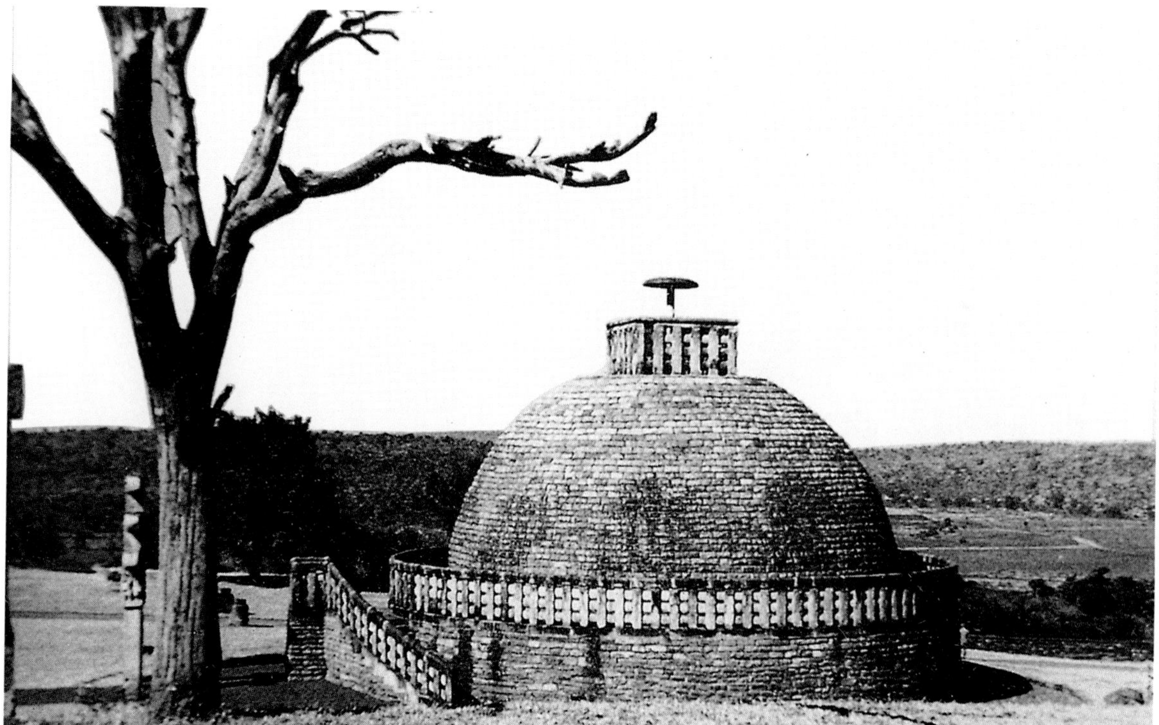

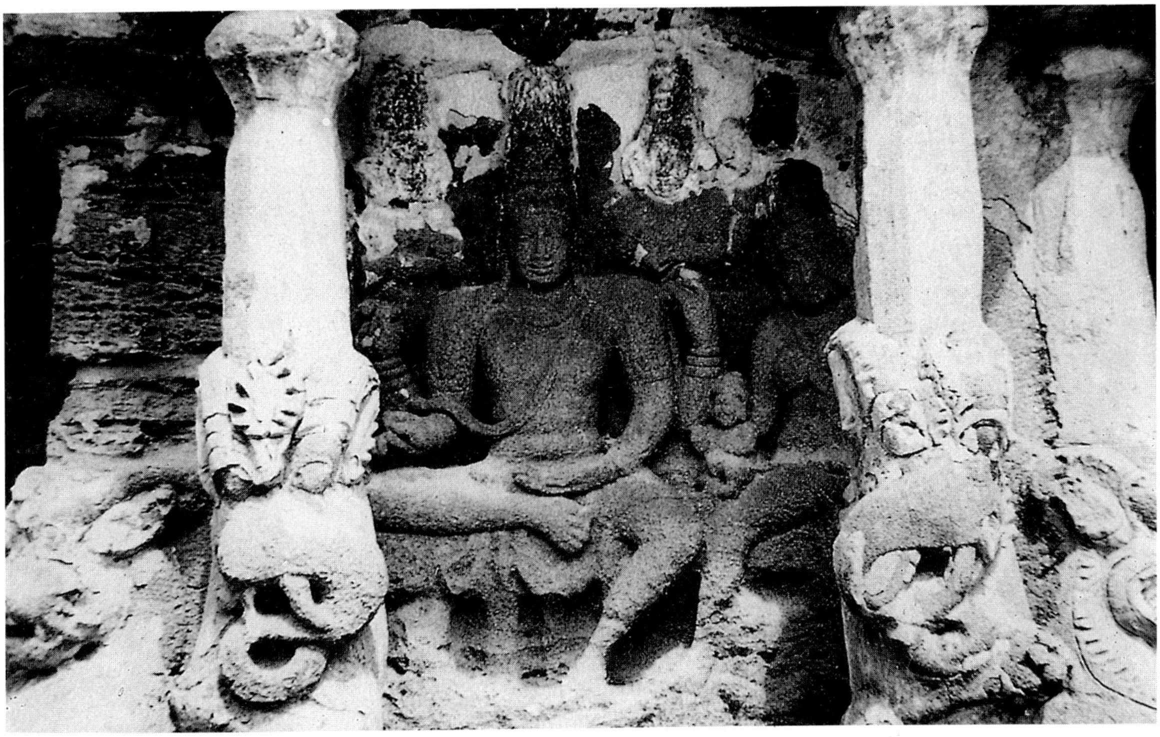

20. Kailasnatha, Kanchi.

20A. Kailasnatha temple, Kanchi.

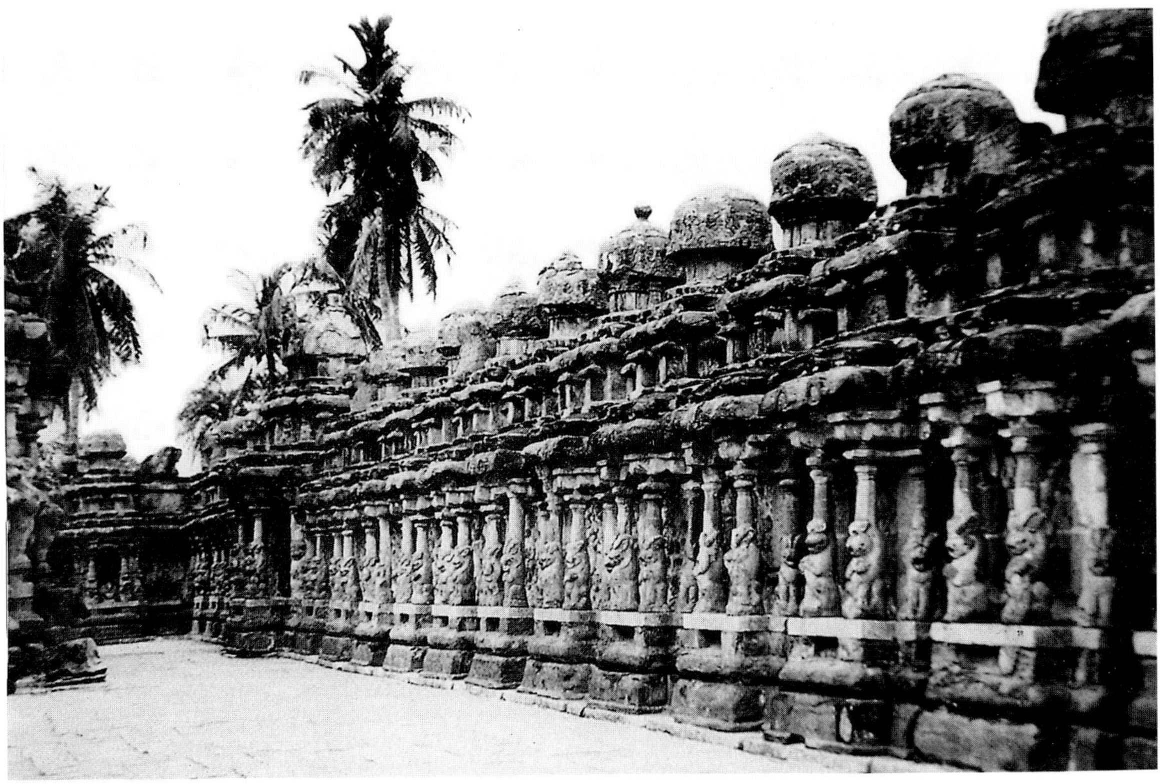

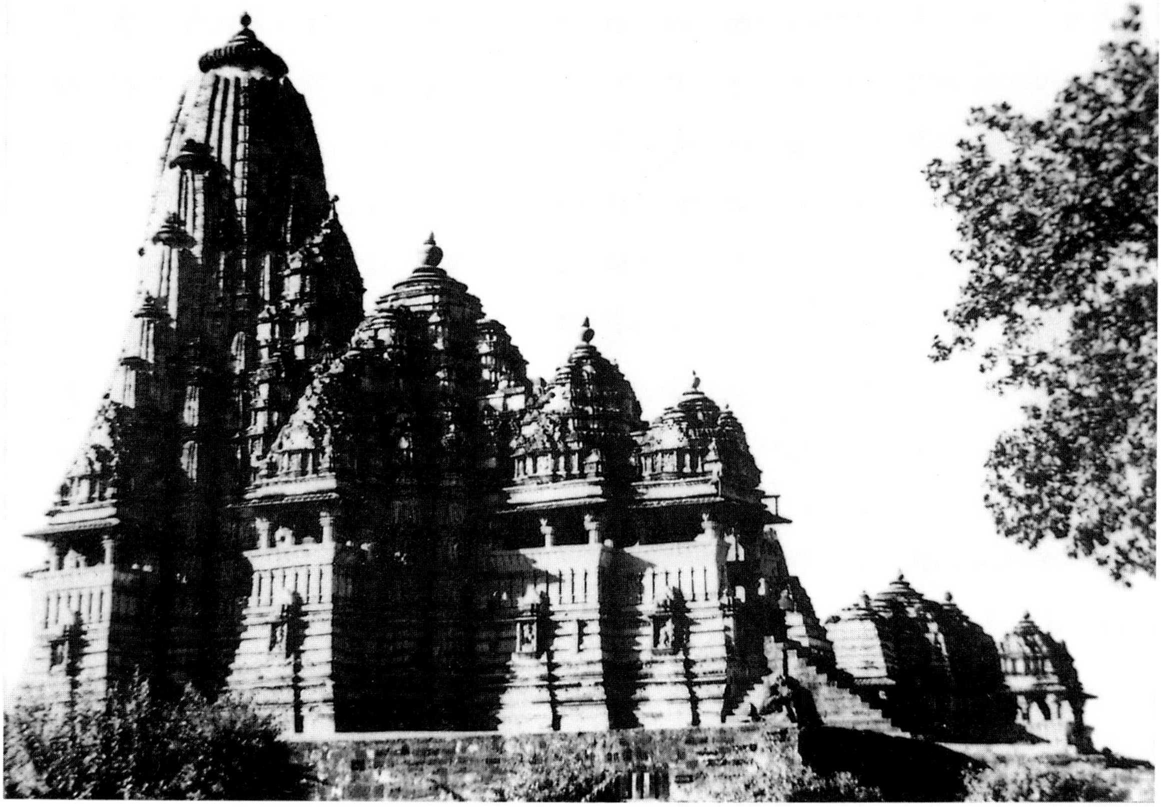

22A. Kandariya Mahadeva temple, Khajuraho.

24A. Airali Durga temple.

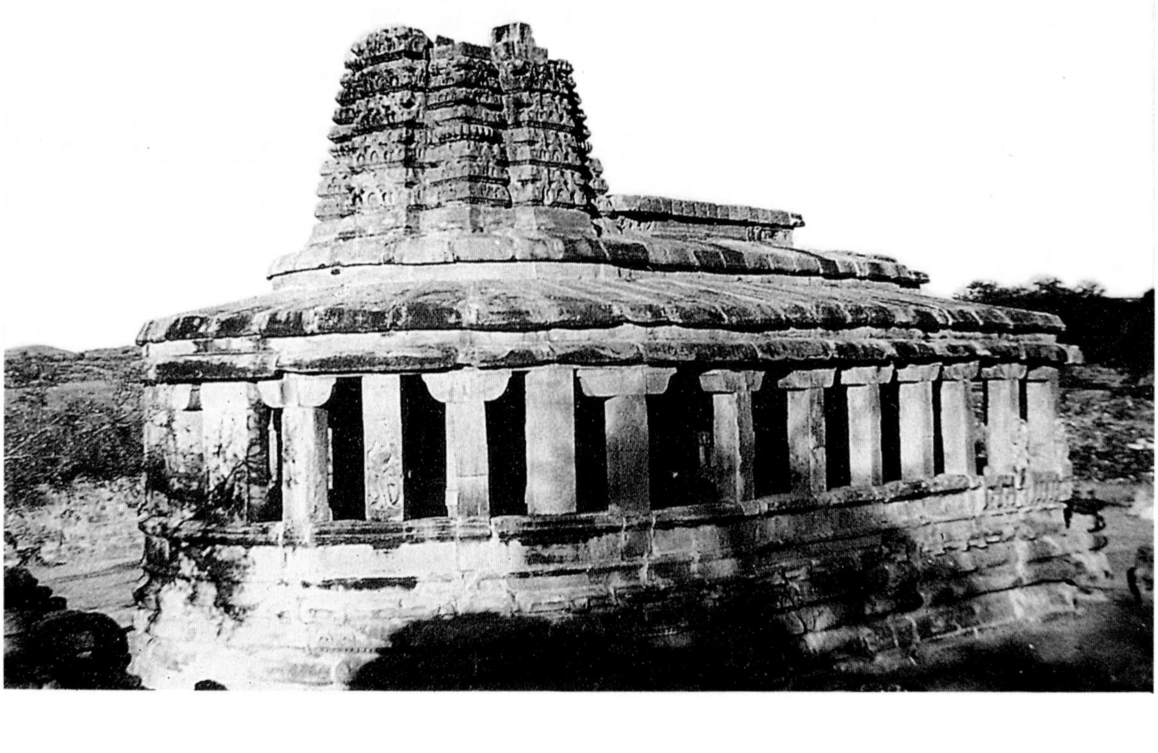

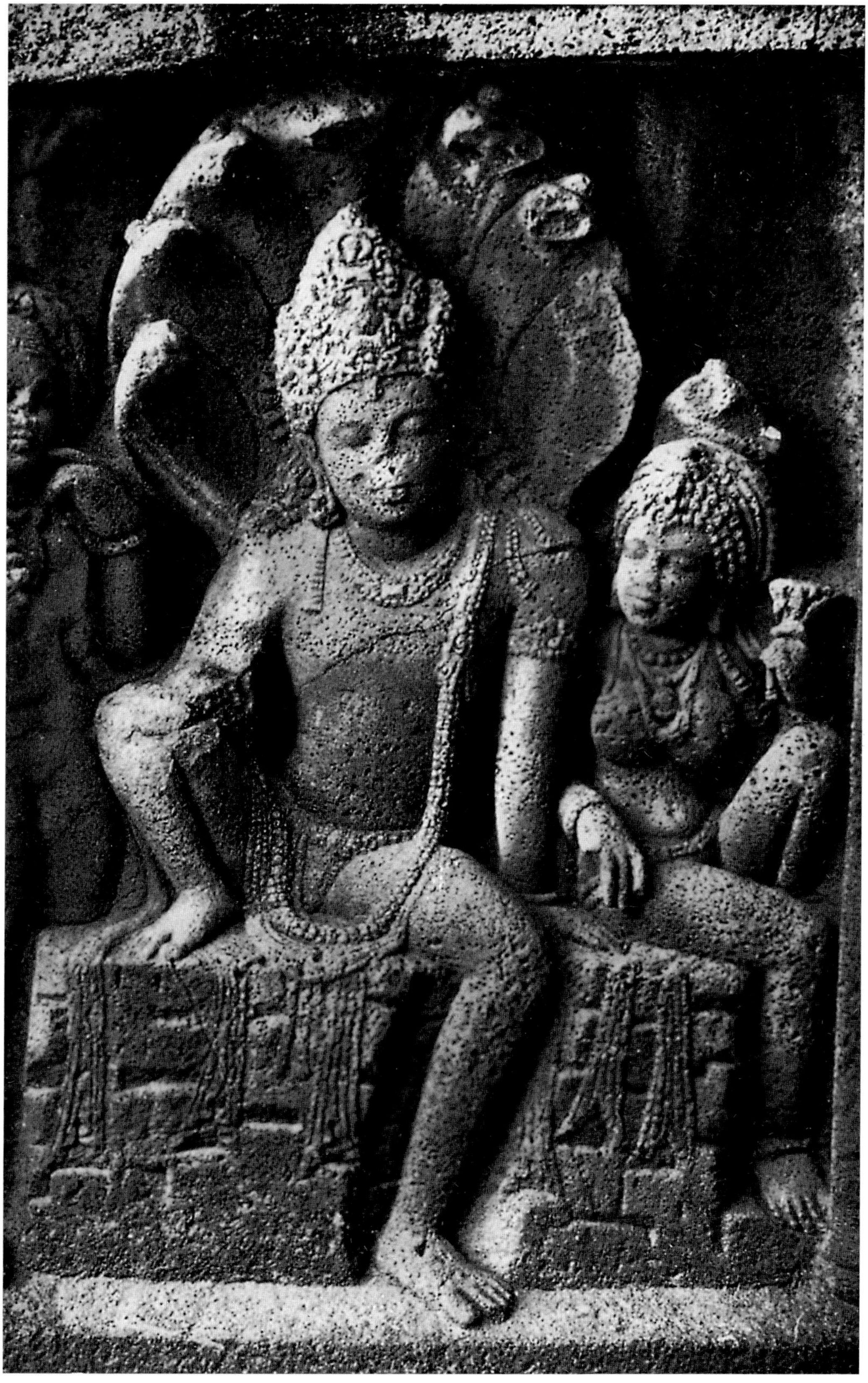

25. Nagaraja and queen, sculpture outside cave 19, Ajanta.

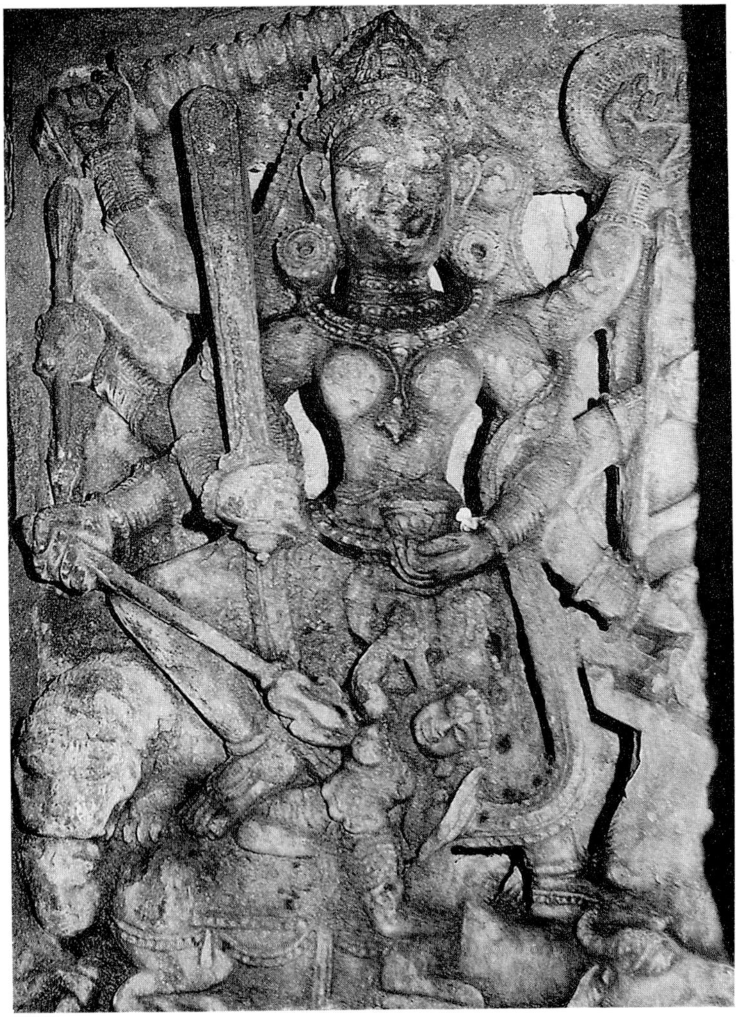

26. Mahishasura Mardini, Chamba temple.

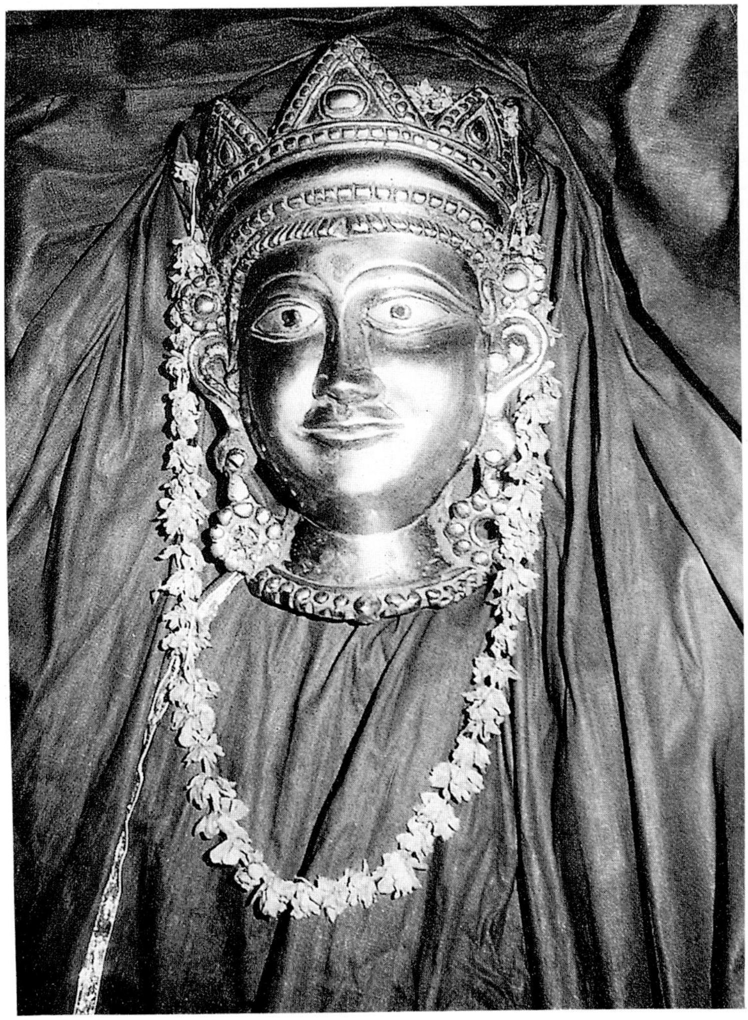

26A. Champa Devi, Chamba temple.

IX

Pattadakkal

Plastic Figures in Pillars and Panels

Along with Badami and Aihole, Pattadakkal constitutes the trinity of Chalukyan legacy in the field of temple architecture and sculpture.

Pattadakkal is 42 miles from Badami and 49 miles from Aihole in Bijapur district of Karnataka. It is a small village located on the banks of the river *Malaprabha*, a tributary of Krishna.

The period of Aihole comes first, Badami next and Pattadakkal last. Though coming broadly under the category of Chalukyan Art, each of these places is significant for its unique contribution.

If Aihole is the birthplace of the **Nagara** type of temple architecture, which found its proliferation in the soaring spires of Bhubaneshwar and Khajuraho, and Badami represents the heralding of the fluent and vibrant treatment of puranic legends, in Pattadakkal, we have beginnings of the Dravidian type of temple architecture—a detailed impress of the Pallava tradition along with the Nagara type of architecture and of a moving rhythm and lightness of sculpture.

Thus, while the *Virupaksha, Sangameswara* and *Mallikarjuna* temples are in the Dravidian style, the *Galagnatha* and *Papanatha* temples are in the Nagara style.

The open location of the temples at Pattadakkal has resulted in the disappearance of valuable works of art and the monuments are in a much less preserved manner than the sculptures in Badami Caves and even the sculptures of the Durga temple at Aihole.

An idea of the present state of Pattadakkal which was once the second capital of the Chalukyas can be had from the following remarks of a local tourist pamphlet:

> **PATTADAKKAL:** Altitude—580 feet; Season—November to March; Rail—the nearest railway station of Badami (29 kms); Accommodation— none. The tourists can stay either at Badami or at Bagalkot and visit Pattadakkal during the day.

The same tourist pamphlet pompously proclaims: "The carvings are astounding for the portrayal of arrested motion. The plasticity of the figures in the pillars and panels reveals the sculptors' rare mastery of the medium and the subject. The sculptures in various temples throw considerable light on the social life of the early Chalukyans. The temples here unfold the graded, chronological growth of different systems of architecture which contributed greatly to artistic glory of India."

The glory of our artistic heritage and the pitiable present-day conditions surrounding many of its moving mementoes including the absolute lack of elementary infrastructural facilities like catering, accommodation etc. make one yearn for the day when the two departments of Archaeology and Tourism will be combined under one Ministry of the Government of India so that not only will greater resources be deployed to keep the monuments in better shape but elementary facilities like lodging and boarding provided to zealous tourists who come to see and take pride in such wondrous monuments as at Pattadakkal.

A few lingering sculptures at Pattadakkal like Siva and Parvati, Ravana lifting Kailasa and Siva (*Virupaksha Temple*), the Flying Couple (*Mallikarjuna Temple*), Bhagiratha and Jahnavi and the sculpted pillars of the Virupaksha Temple deserve comment and special appreciation.

While looking at them, one is reminded of the truth of the observations made by Dr. Nihar Ranjan Ray, the famous art historian: "Towards the middle of the eighth century the reliefs of the temples of Pattadakkal reflect the impress of the South Indian tradition of Mamallapuram and Kanchipuram right from Deccanese inheritance. Sculptures are not fully blended into a creative synthesis. The figures attain a slender suppleness and elegance so characteristic of the south of a previous age. The easy, silent and graceful movements add charm to the artistic dignity and proportion in not a few of the panels marked in high relief. Indeed much more refined and elevated in taste and serious and condensed in spirit, the Pattadakkal reliefs lift to a much higher level the light and thin plastic conceptions of the south."

The elegant diminutive depiction of Ravana lifting Kailasa is pleasantly different from its counterpart in Ellora, where the sculpture is, no doubt, massive and forceful. The Siva-Parvati panel bears the clear impress of Pallava style, the unique feature being the insertion of the bull in between like a pet puppy. The decorative element characteristic of Chalukyan sculpture is visible in *Bhagiratha* and *Jahnavi* temples as also the sculpted pillar in Virupaksha temple.

Siva standing majestically trampling the elephant is a masterpiece, exuding charm, grace and elegance. The female figures in Pattadakkal, however, have not attained the grace of the later Khajuraho figures.

Pattadakkal was the melting pot in which the heavy Deccanese style started merging with the light Southern style. To quote Dr. Nihar Ranjan Ray again, "The process at work in Pattadakkal reached maturity at Ellora in the Kailasnath Temple and the creative fusion of concentrated and sustained power and heaviness of form of the Deccan and of ease, grace and suppleness of the South resulted in mighty carvings of forceful movement and noble and dignified elegance blended into one."

X

Elephanta

Epiphany of Indian Genius

"Where the Elephanta Temple is superior to all others of its kind is in the character and quality of its sculptures, particularly on the back or the southern wall. Here are three large square recesses, divided off by pilasters each of which bears a gigantic figure of a *dwarpala*. The panel to the left or east contains a spirited representation of *ardhanari*, a manifestation of Siva typifying the male and female energies, while the corresponding panel on the right enshrines figures of Siva, *Maheshmurti*, is the creation of a genius.

"Few works of sculpture excel the magnificent treatment of this colossal triple bust in which the whole essence of the creed is concentrated in forms of marvellous refinement and subtlety, curved, and full, and alive; *in the white heat of passion, the sculptor seems to have melted the very substance of the rock and infused into it something of his own soul.*" Thus observes Percy Brown in his monumental work *Indian Architecture.*

The Elephanta Caves are in the green islands of Elephanta, so called after the huge statue of an elephant (now in Victoria Gardens, Bombay) which once stood there, which lies six miles across the Bombay harbour.

From the Gateway of India, it takes one hour by boat to reach the island and a few minutes walk uphill to reach the cave temple.

The caves were excavated between the sixth and eighth centures A.D. during the reign of Vakatakas in the Deccan, who ruled during the same period when the Imperial Guptas flourished in the North, and could be contemporaneous with some of the caves of Ellora and Ajanta.

Invading Portuguese soldiers have damaged many of the sculpture pieces but not succeeded in destroying their beauty.

Some tourist guide books consider the sculpture at Elephanta "meagre fare" compared to Ellora and Ajanta. Such comparisons are odious. It is not bulk that matters.

The unique contribution of Elephanta is the "*Maheshmurti*", (the Supreme God) also known as "*Trimurti*", in which the Indian sculptor has projected the Upanishadic concept of one God, combining in Himself the task of creation, preservation and destruction.

Many art critics have burst into superlative eulogies about the *Trimuti* of Elephanta.

Dr. Rene Grousset writes: "The *Maheshmurti*, the three-headed bust at Elephanta is perhaps the greatest masterpiece of the world's art. The three countenances of the one being are here harmonised without a trace of effort. There are few material representations of the divine principle at once so powerful and so balanced as this, in the art of the whole world. Nay, more: here we have undoubtedly the grandest representation of the Pantheist God ever made by the hand of man."

Kulapati Munshi has observed: "Indeed, never have the exuberant vigour of life, the tumult for universal joy expressing itself in ordered harmony, the pride of power superior to any other, and the secret exaltation of the divinity immanent in all things, found such serene expression. In its Olympian majesty, the *Maheshmurti* of Elephanta is worthy of comparison with the *Zeus* of *Mylasa* or the *Askleopios* of *Melos.*"

Any amount of description in words or any number of photographs cannot be a substitute for the actual experience of standing before this magnificent, colossal artistic creation of Indian genius and feeling the sublimity, serenity and majesty of God, the Supreme Creator, Preserver and Destroyer.

Next to the main Maheshmurti image, the most important sculptural panels are those of the *Ardhanareeswara* Siva, in which Siva has absorbed unto himself half the body of his spouse, Parvati, and the marriage of *Siva* with *Parvati.*

The concept of *Ardhanareeswara,* like that of Trimurti, is again peculiar to the Indian genius. It symbolises, as one writer put it, "the unity of the male and female elements in the universe."

Ardhanareeswara literally means, in Sanskrit, "The Lord who is half woman." This concept must be music to ears of feminists in the West who are seriously debating whether God is man or woman.

Indian genius rightly recognises the equality of men and women and their equal importance as "partners of creation". United they create, divided and confronting and competing with each other, they perish.

The marriage of *Siva* and *Parvati* is a theme which has inspired poets, artists and sculptors in India to the highest levels of creative excellence, throughout her history.

Kalidasa's "Kumarasambhava" is a classic example, as are the thrilling sculptures in caves 16, 21 and 29 at Ellora.

The Elephanta panel is also exquisite, portraying expressively the coy, yet happy bride and the majestic bridegroom. The figures carved by the Ellora sculptors are massive and awe-inspiring, while those in Elephanta are more youthful, delicate and elegant.

The other panels at Elephanta depict the famous legends linked with Siva in Puranic mythology like the descent of the *Ganges,* the killing of the demon *Andhaka,* and the dance of *Siva* as *Nataraja.*

These legends which have become part of the racial memory of Indians, merit a brief mention, for the benefit of those not fully familiar with details so that the sculptor's skill shown at Elephanta is better understood.

Sagara, the Ikshvaku ruler, wanting to perform the asvamedha sacrifice, set loose a horse with auspicious marks, accompanied by his sons and a well equipped army. Indra, afraid of a threat to his sovereignty, stole the horse and left it in the hermitage of Kapila, who was promptly attacked by Sagara's sons. The enraged Kapila reduced Sagara's sons to ashes.

Attempts were made to revive the dead by trying to bring the heavenly Ganga to the earth. Sagara's grandson Ansuman and his son Dilipa both failed in the attempt. Ultimately, Dilipa's son Bhagiratha did severe penance and got the blessing that Ganga would descend to the earth, but subject to the condition that the descent should be broken lest the earth should get washed away.

The Lord to whom Bhagiratha prayed, agreed to receive the turbulent Ganga in his matted locks and allowed her to flow gently to the earth over the ashes of Sagara's sons, who immediately came back to life. As a result of this feat, the Lord came to be known as *Gangadhara*, "The one who holds Ganga (in his matted locks)".

The destruction of the demon *Andhaka* is symbolic of divine intervention, when arrogance and evil raise their heads and oppress the world. Andhaka, the son of sage Kashyapa, became all powerful and going to Kailasa tried to carry away Parvati. The Lord destroyed the arrogant Andhaka, using Vishnu's discus and protected the world.

The dance of Siva has been interpreted in diverse ways. Dr. Ananda Coomaraswamy exclaims: "The essential significance of Siva's dance is threefold: first, it is the image of His rhythmic play as a source of all movement within the cosmos, secondly, the purpose of His dance is to release the countless souls of men from the snare of illusion, thirdly, the place of the dance, *Chidambaram*, the centre of the universe, is within the heart."

The colossal figure of Siva Nataraja at Elephanta, though broken, is full of movement "suggesting the emanation of cosmic forces."

Some of the sculpture pieces from Elephanta have been removed to various museums. A particularly beautiful piece the five-headed Sadasiva may be seen in the Prince of Wales Museum, Bombay.

At one end of the main cave is a shrine, guarded on all the four sides by eight handsome *dwarpalas*. In the sanctum sanctorum, a *lingam* has been installed.

The *lingam* as a symbol of the all-pervading God, the Lord of all creation, evokes in the Indian mind feelings of reverence and devotion. The westerners with their mental hangups are open to see phallic connections in the *lingam*. But such ideas do not occur in the minds of the Indian devotee, to whom the *lingam* is a sacred symbol of the Lord. In fact after one sees the *lingam* at Elephanta, and comes out, one can see right across the sea on the shore another *lingam*, the dome-shaped Cyrus Atomic Reactor which also is a symbol of energy, creation and destruction.

There are also panels at Elephanta depicting *Ganesha*, *Kumara* and *Ravana* trying to lift *Kailasa*, and *Siva* as the meditating yogi.

A visit to Elephanta is a deep spiritual experience. Standing inside the cave before the various panels depicting the legends describing the glory of the Lord and enjoying reverentially the majesty and grandeur of the *Maheshmurti*, one is reminded of the verses from the *Svetasvatara Upanishad* which proclaim the glory of the Supreme Lord:

Ya yékóvarnó bahudhā śakti yógāt
varnān anékān nihitārthó dadhāti,
Vicaiti cāntó viśwamādau ca dévaḥ
sa nó buddhyā śubhayā samyunaktu.

य एकोऽवर्णो बहुधा शक्तियोगाद्
वर्णाननेकान् निहितार्थो दधाति।
विचैति चान्तो विश्वमादौ च देव:
स नो बुद्धया शुभया संयुनक्तु॥

"Let the God, the unique one, the indefinable one, who, by his union with Sakti, assumes, without any self-interest, myriad forms, first creates the universe and then at the end, withdraws it into himself, bestow on us good intellects."

Sa tanmayó hyamṛta īśa samsthó
gnaḥ sarvagó bhuvanasyāsya góptā,
Ya īśósya jagató nityaméva
nānyó heturvidyata īśanāya.

स तन्मयो ह्यमृत ईश संस्थो
ज्ञ: सर्वगो भुवनस्यास्य गोप्ता।
य ईशोऽस्य जगतो नित्यमेव
नान्यो हेतु र्विद्यत ईशनाय॥

"The Lord is the essence of the universe. He is immortal, omniscient, omnipresent keeper of the universe. He is the permanent Lord of the universe, none else."

Tamīśwarāṇām paramam mahéśwaram
devatānām paramam ca daivatam,
Patim patīnām paramam parastāt
vidāma dévam bhuvanéśamīdyam.

तमीश्वराणां परमं महेश्वरं
देवतानां परमं च दैवतम्।
पतिं पतीनां परमं परस्ताद्
विदाम देवं भुवनेशमीड्यम्॥

"May we realise Him—the transcendent and adorable Master of the universe—who is the Supreme Lord over all the lords, the Supreme God of all the gods, the Supreme Ruler over all the rulers."

XI

Ellora

Eulogy to Divinity

"It is a great spiritual achievement..., an illustration of one of those rare occasions when men's minds, hearts and hands work in unison towards the consummation of an ideal." These remarks of Percy Brown made with reference to Kailasa temple, one of the caves of Ellora, can apply to the whole of Ellora itself.

If there is one place of pilgrimage to which every Indian should pay a visit to recharge his national ego, it is Ellora.

The caves of Ellora, 34 in number, have been carved out of a sloping mountain (called Elapura, hence the name Ellora), unlike those at Ajanta, where the cliff is perpendicular. Of these, 12 are Buddhist caves, five Jain and the remaining 17 are Hindu caves. The Buddhist caves were exacavated between 450 A.D. and 642 A.D., the Hindu caves between the 7 and 8th centuries and the Jain temples between the 9th and 11th centuries.

The Hindu caves predominate in volume and spirit at Ellora. The recurring theme dealt with by the anonymous artists and artisans is the love and marriage of Siva and Parvati, the Divine Parents—a theme which has haunted the imagination of poets, down the centuries. What Kalidasa, Pushpadanta and Sankara have painted in poetry has been carved out in Ellora.

The Siva-Sakti theme has been dealt with in art and sculpture at various places, during various periods of India's history under the patronage of various rulers: the Guptas, the Pallavas, the Chalukyas, the Cholas, the Pratiharas, the Vakatakas, the Chandellas, etc. But the way it has been dealt with at Ellora is unique.

As Michael Edwardes writes in his book, *Indian Temples and Palaces,* "The Ellora caves convey a tremendous sense of divine in the figures of gods. They are aloof and spiritual. The sculptor's treatment is not 'realistic', and for all the solidity of the stone in which they are carved, the figures give the impression that they are merely appearances, insubstantial and visual projections of God's presence."

The most impressive among the Ellora caves is the *Kailasa* temple (cave 16). The celestial abode of Siva, the Auspicious One, has been sought to be recreated on earth. It is perhaps the grandest monolithic excavation in the world. The architects worked from above downwards until they struck a gigantic solid rock which they shaped into a temple.

It took 100 years to complete the Kailasa temple which was started under the patronage of the Rashtrakuta King, Krishna I.

The wealth of sculpture carved out at the Kailasa temple has to be seen to be believed. Siva and Parvati in various poses, scenes depicting their marriage, Ravana trying to lift Kailasa and the celestial dance of Siva watched by the Ganas and Ganesha and the *Paisachas,** are imposing in their majesty and fascinating in their beauty of conception. They send cold shivers of thrill in the Indian spectator.

A copper plate inscription relating to the reign of King Krishna I vividly describes the glory of the Kailasa in these words: "Krishnaraja caused to be constructed a temple of wonderful form on the mountain of Elapura (Ellora). When the gods moving in their aerial cars saw it, they were struck with wonder and constantly thought of it saying to themselves: 'This temple of Siva must have created itself, for such beauty is not to be found in a work of art.' Even the architect who created it was struck with wonder. His heart failed him when it considered building another like it, for 'how is it possible that I built except by magic?'"

Though Kailasa or cave 16 is the **piece de resistance** of Ellora, caves 14, 15, 21 and 29 also offer a surfeit of sculpture, depicting the various legends revolving round Siva. Of those cave 29 displays

*Ghostly spirits.

gigantic figures. Siva's marriage with Parvati depicted in this cave (150 feet wide) is awe-inspiring and recalls to one's mind its description by Kalidasa in the seventh canto of **Kumarasambhava**. The scene beautifully shows Siva holding the hand of His Bride, in the presence of the distinguished gathering which included Vishnu, Brahma (seated in front of the fire and the galaxy of celestials like Indra, riding His elephant, the seven sacred sages (**Saptarishis**), the *Ganas,** etc.

As Kalidasa remarks:

Prayukta pāṇigrahaṇam yadanyadvadhūvaram puṣyati
Kāntimagrāmasānnidhya yogādanayostadānīm
Kim kathyate śrīrubhayasya tasya.

—verse 78, 7th canto, *Kumarasambhavam*

प्रयुक्त पाणिग्रहणं यदन्यद्वधूवरं पुष्यति
कान्तिमग्रामसान्निध्य योगादनयोस्तदानीम्
किं कथ्यते श्रीरुभयस्य तस्य॥

"Siva and Parvati, when invoked in marriages, render resplendent earthly couples, how can one describe the radiance of the couple, when they themselves were getting married?"

The art of the Ellora sculptor competes competently with the poetic skill of Kalidasa.

Ravana trying to lift Kailasa is a depiction repeated in caves 14, 16 and 21. One cannot improve on Fodor's description of this outstanding work of art: "You can almost feel the mountain tremble in this piece of sculpture, but you are reassured by the unperturbed figure of Siva who is taking care of His downstairs neighbour by merely putting His foot down so hard that Ravana is caught below. Parvati seems to be a little preoccupied: She clings to Her Husband's arm as any young wife would in a similar situation."

The Buddhist caves at Ellora are similar to the caves at Ajanta, with seated Buddhas and large *Chaityas* (Monasteries).

Of the five Jain caves, cave 32 is most outstanding and is known as the "*Indrasabha*". Intricate workmanship and meticulous

*Spiritual attendants.

carving notwithstanding, these caves cannot stand comparison with the caves 16, 21 and 29.

When one returns from a visit to Ellora, what stands out in one's memory is the tribute to Divinity that the sculptors have paid with their chisel and hammer—a tribute soaked in mythological memory, and offered in pious devotion.

Standing before the awe-inspiring images in the Kaiḷasa temple and cave 29, one could not help making a mental comparison between Khajuraho and Ellora. Notwithstanding the soaring spires, the flesh is predominant in the sculptured figures of Khajuraho. Ellora on the other hand is out and out a monument to the spirit.

The spirit in Ellora has easily triumphed over the flesh in Khajuraho.

XII

Ajanta

The Attic of Buddhist Art

"If you could imagine an earth-moving feat on the scale of the pyramids, a flowering of sculpture and painting worthy of the renaissance and a religious fervour as intense as that of medieval Europe, you might begin to have an idea of the cave temples at Ellora and Ajanta." This is how Fodor's guide to India introduces the Ajanta and Ellora caves to its readers.

Though the Ajanta and Ellora caves are often mentioned together, and both are located in Maharashtra State, they are 45 miles away from each other and the easily accessible points of entry are different. Ajanta caves are 37 miles from *Jalagaon,* a railway station on the Bombay-Delhi route. Ellora caves are only 20 miles from *Aurangabad,* which is connected by air from both Delhi and Bombay.

One feels symptomatically sad to learn that the Ajanta caves, the pride of India and human civilisation, carved out nearly 300 years ago, between 200 B.C. and 650 A.D., were unknown in the country of its origin till a hundred and odd years back (1819), when they were accidentally discovered by a shooting party of British soldiers.

Historically, these caves are associated with the Vakataka dynasty, vassals of the Great Guptas, who ruled supreme in India between 320 and 495 A.D.

The golden age of the Guptas was, no doubt, a period of renaissance in Indian art, sculpture and literature, and many of the

Ajanta paintings and sculptures fall during this period. But the fact that quite a few were created in earlier periods and some even in the first and second century B.C. indicates a high level of creative power even before the Guptas.

The Ajanta caves are entirely Buddhist and the themes dealt with by the artists and sculptors revolve round the life of the Buddha and the legends of the *Jataka* stories.

There are in all 30 caves, of which five are *Chaityas* or chapels and the rest are *Viharas* or monasteries. Natural light gets into most of these caves at given times of the day. The facade and the interior are decorated with sculpture and the walls inside contain the frescoes or paintings.

The *raison d'être* of cave sculpture and painting often dazes the visitor. Why did the Buddhist monks seek out these inaccessible mountain rocks for their artistic expression? The answer is simple. Rock architecture was preferred because of readily available rocks, which have a permanent durability. Also, asceticism and monastic life induced people to retire into secluded mountain resorts where they could give unfettered expression to their creative impulses, secure in the belief that their artistic creations would be free from intrusions of marauding invaders.

Among the Ajanta caves the most important are caves 1, 2, 4, 10, 16, 17, 19, 24 and 26.

The facade of the first cave contains six carved pillars. Inside is a huge seated Buddha in meditation, whose expression changes according to the light and angle from sorrow to peace and to smile.

One of the paintings in cave one depicts the *Sibi story*: how a pigeon fleeing from a hawk sought refuge in the king and how the king protected the pigeon by giving the hawk his own flesh, equivalent in weight to that of the pigeon.

There are panels of paintings depicting Buddha's life. In one painting four deer share one head. The painted panel on the ceiling shows elephants, flowers and dwarfs.

There are two masterpieces in cave one: one is of *Padmapani*, which depicts the Bodhisattva, with flower in hand, on the way to enlightenment, the other of *Vajrapani*, a bejewelled Bodhisattva. There is also the portrait of the black princess.

Cave two contains paintings related to the birth of the Buddha.

Cave four contains some sculptures, while cave 10 is an imposing *Chaitya* (Monastery), the oldest cave, dating back to the second century B.C.

Cave 16 contains the famous *Dying Princess,* which shows Sundari, the wife of Buddha's cousin Nanda who deserted her to become a Buddhist monk.

In cave 17 one sees the largest number of unspoilt paintings which indicate the wealth of life lived by the people of ancient India. In these paintings of princes, princesses and the common people, one finds hair styles which could put to shame the most modern coiffures, dress designs which are borrowed by modern imitators, necklaces which are a jeweller's delight, and footwear and handbags one would least expect to find so many centuries ago, but which are proof positive of the sophisticated civilisation of ancient India.

One of the tenderest paintings of cave 17 is *Mother and Child before Buddha,* when Buddha returns as a mendicant, seeking alms, to his wife and child. Buddha is depicted as a towering figure in this painting.

Caves 19, 24 and 26 mainly have sculptures. One of the famous among these is that of *Nagaraja and Queen* in a niche outside cave 19. The facades and the interior also have some large Buddhas which is a splendid achievement of Mahayana Buddhism which sought to see in Buddha an incarnation of God.

A visit to the Ajanta caves is a purifying experience. While one wonders at the artistic vision and the supreme technical skill of the artists and craftsmen of ancient India who produced this marvel, one feels the profound impact of Buddhist philosophy in the art of Ajanta.

As the introduction of the UNESCO Publication on Ajanta paintings points out: "Human life, in the crowded drama of love, compassion, happiness, yearning, death, suffering and sacrifice, is illuminated by a glow of religious feeling dominated by a sense of transience of existence and profound piety...In the intermingling of human beings, plants, flowers and animals there is a feeling of deep and intimate spiritual kinship among all forms of life."

The art of India has always been tempered by religion, yet the creative genius of India has a unifying and undying quality which cuts across religion. This would be evident to anyone who sees and compares the triumphant flowering of Indian art, whether in the

Buddhist caves of Ajanta, the Hindu caves of Ellora, the Jain temples of Dilwara or the Muslim monuments of Agra and Fatehpur Sikri.

But for the present, we are at Ajanta, feasting our eyes on the paintings and sculptures while our minds muse about the *Jataka* stories and meditate on Buddha, the great Renouncer.

XIII

Nalanda

Nerve Centre of Buddhist Learning

Whenever I arrive at a new place, the first thing I get acquainted with is the origin of the name of the place. So, as soon as I reached the ruins at Nalanda, travelling 65 miles by road from Gaya, the famous tourist centre, I asked the tourist guide the usual question: "Why is Nalanda called Nalanda?" He could give me no answer.

I checked with the tourist booklets and found the following three plausible answers. One: Buddha as a Bodhisattva in a previous birth was the ruler of the place and was so charitable that he never said to anyone who approached him: "I shall not give" (*na alam da*) (in Pali or Sanskrit) from which we have *Nalanda*.

Second: The place is full of lotus pools. *Nala* in Sanskrit means lotus, hence Nalanda.

Third: Nalanda is the name of the Naga who lived in the lake nearby.

Nalanda was only a suburb of Rajgir, the ancient Magadhan capital city, the first recorded capital of India and a flourishing city in 6th century B.C. It was full of mango groves. Buddha used to stop at Nalanda on his way to and from Rajgir. Nalanda also acquired sanctity as the birthplace of Sariputta, chief disciple of Buddha.

Though Asoka is believed to have built a stupa at Nalanda and some kind of a study centre might have existed at Nalanda during the first four centuries after Christ, enriched by the association of scholars like Nagarjuna, Aryadeva, Asanga Vasubandhu and Dinnaga, and by the great university in Nalanda, with the attendant monasteries, the ruins of which are seen today, it is considered by experts to date back only to the period of the later Guptas, in the fifth and sixth centuries A.D.

Hiuen Tsang, the Chinese pilgrim, writes in his *chronicles* that Narasimhagupta Baladitya "after having vanquished all the foes and enjoyed the entire earth erected a great and extraordinary temple at Nalanda." He also refers to Sakraditya having built a monastery. Sakraditya's successors like Buddhagupta, Tathagatagupta, Baladitya and Vajra are also mentioned as builders of Monasteries at Nalanda.

Harsha was also a great patron of the great university of Nalanda, which, by then, had become the most renowned centre of learning in the whole of the Buddhist world.

A better description of the glory that was Nalanda cannot be found than the one in Bhavan's *History and Culture of the Indian People, Volume Three: The Classical Age* (pp. 585-586):

> "Nalanda in Magadha was renowned alike for the magnificence of its establishment and the intellectual and moral pre-eminence of its inmates. Owing its foundations to six successive generations of Gupta kings, it housed a population of several thousands who were maintained out of the revenues of a hundred (or more) villages, specially endowed for its upkeep. The resident monks were esteemed not only for their learning but also for their high character so much so that they were, according to Hiuen Tsang, looked up to as models all over India.
>
> "Because of its fame, Nalanda attracted students from abroad, but so strict was the examination test that only two or three out of ten succeeded in getting admission. The monks spent their time wholly on study and debates and the monastery had a long list of alumni to its credit.
>
> "According to Hiuen Tsang, the buildings consisted of eight halls besides the great college and according to I-Tsing, eight halls with three hundred apartments."

The ruins at Nalanda vouch for the substantial correctness of the Chinese pilgrims. The only rival of Nalanda as a centre of learning in India in the seventh century was Valabhi in Kathiawar.

The curriculum of studies in Nalanda comprised not only the works of all the 18 schools of Buddhism, but also the four *Vedas*, the six *Vedangas*, *Puranas*, *Nyaya*, *Mimamsa*, *Dharmasastra*, *Dhanurveda*,

Gandharvaveda, Arthasastra, Hetuvidya (Logic), *Sabdavidya* (grammar), *Chikitsavidya* (Medicine), *Atharvavidya, Sānkhya,* etc.

The Pali rulers who ruled Eastern India from the eighth century to the twelfth century continued to patronise the University of Nalanda and gave generous grants.

One inscription records that Nalanda was built in the latter half of the tenth century by King Mahipala after destruction by fire. During 1197-1203 A.D. Bakhtiyar Khilji destroyed Nalanda and set fire to all the libraries, monasteries and stupas. For seven years Nalanda remained neglected.

In 1860, Alexander Cunningham, the great archaeologist, rediscovered Nalanda and excavations by the archaeological department brought to light the monuments in ruins.

These, though few in number, will give us an idea of the glory that was once Nalanda.

The biggest surviving monument is the great stupa flanked by flights of steps and terraces. Remnants of monasteries can also be seen, where the students used to stay and study.

The nearby museum contains many sculpture pieces excavated from the site. Prominent among these are: bronze statues of Buddha, Bodhisattvas and serpent-hooded goddesses.

A visit to Nalanda is an elevating experience. After a somewhat tiring round of the expansive ruins, one can visualise in one's mental vision what the "most magnificent temple of learning in Jambudweepa" (to borrow the epithet of the Chinese pilgrim, I-Tsing) would have looked like in its heyday of glory which spanned ten centuries.

Fifteen hundred teachers! Ten thousand students drawn from all parts of the country and abroad! An invaluable collection of books and manuscripts! Excellent facilities for boarding and lodging! Perfect discipline maintained democratically by the alumni! What more could one hope for in an academy of learning? Silabhadra, the great Chancellor! An assembly of great minds like Hiuen Tsang, Chandra Pala, Prabhamitra, Jinamitra, Jinachandra and so on! And the profound study of Brahminical and Buddhist, sacred and secular, science and philosophy, Metaphysics and Mythology, Art and Grammar, Logic and Medicine!

How green was Nalanda then!

XIV

Konarak

Kalinga Art at its Zenith

"A vision in stone of the chariot of the sun." That is how Zimmer refers to the famous sun temple at Konarak which foreigners have also referred to as the "*Black Pagoda*", since, to mariners at sea, it looked like a black mass, as compared to the white of the Puri temple.

In the Hindu pantheon, six deities command widespread worship: **Siva, Sakti, Vishnu, Ganesha, Kumara** and **Surya** (the sun). Worshippers of these deities have evolved clearly defined modes of worship and temples have been raised in their honour throughout the country down the centuries.

While temples dedicated to other deities are prolific in number, the ones dedicated to the sun are very few: the most important being the one in **Martand** in Kashmir (built in the eighth century A.D.), the **Modhera** temple in Gujarat (eleventh century) and the **Konarak** temple (built in the thirteenth century).

Konarak is 40 miles by road, southeast of Bhubaneshwar, the capital of Orissa (which has an airport and a railhead). From Puri it is 50 miles by road.

In Sanskrit, **Kona** means angle and **Arka** means sun. Thus Konarak means "the angle of the sun".

The Konarak temple appears to have been built during the reign of the Ganga ruler, Narasimha Deva (1238-1264 A.D.). It marks the culmination of the Kalinga style of temple architecture which flourished in Orissa from the tenth century to the thirteenth century A.D.

The temple construction took years for completion. It is truly one of the great wonders of India. Percy Brown remarked (with a tinge of exaggeration) that had the early European visitors reached Konarak just about the time they saw the Taj Mahal, they would have put Konarak and not the Taj Mahal as one of the seven wonders of the world.

Here is the encomium on Konarak: "Few buildings can boast of such unrestrained abundance of plastic decoration as this vast structure, every portion of the exterior being moulded and chiselled either in the form of abstract geometrical ornament, conventional foliage, mythical animals, fabulous beings, half-human with half-serpent coil, figures satanic, figures divine, of every conceivable motif and subject, known to the human mind and in a technique which ranges from patterns cut with minute precision of a cameo to powerfully modelled groups of colossal size."

The chief architect of the sun temple was *Sibai Santra.* There is a story as to how, after laying the foundation stone of the temple, he roamed about the seashore, racking his brain to find out the best method of erecting the edifice.

He went off to sleep on the sandy seashore and was woken up by an old woman, who offered him hot porridge to eat. Ravenously hungry, he started taking the porridge from the middle of the plate and naturally burnt his fingers in the process. The old woman remarked: "Your manner of eating is like Sibai Santra's manner of building the temple. You must start from the edge and not dip your finger in it as he throws stones into the middle." Sibai Santra took the cue and built the temple accordingly.

The whole temple was built in the form of a huge chariot of the sun drawn by seven horses, with twelve beautifully carved pairs of wheels, each wheel representing a month of the year, seven horses presumably symbolising the seven days of the week.

Unfortunately, the temple is in ruins now. Only the mandapa remains, the main structure, the **sikhara** falling to pieces. On the lintel, which once supported the eastern doorway, were carved the nine grahas (important in astrology): the Sun, Moon, Mars, Mercury, Jupiter, Venus, Saturn and the two nodes: Rahu and Ketu.

Life statues of the sun god and his charioteer have been carved on three sides of the main temple.

Adorning the top floors of the *mandapa* (known as **jagamohana**) is the **natamandir** (the dance-hall) with four entrances and beautifully carved pillars. The *natamandir* and the *jagamohana* were so juxtaposed that at sunrise the first rays used to pierce the interior of the dance-hall and light up the mandapa.

The approach to the *natamandir* is flanked by two figures of lions rampant upon prostrate elephants.

By the side of the main edifice stand two elephants and two horses on broad platforms.

One cannot improve upon Kulapati Munshi's description of the horses at Konarak: "The front hooves of the horses plunge cruelly upon a fallen warrior who holds up a shield in desperation, his face portraying the greatest anguish. A rider stands beside each horse, sword in hand, in a pose suggestive of pride and victory. These horses have been carved with unique vitality."

Sculpture at Konarak is a feast for the eyes. Carved from the most gigantic size to almost miniature figures, fitted into almost inconceivable niches, these figures almost exploit to the full the beautiful feminine figure and all the teachings of the **Kamasutra** and the **Natyasastra**.

To quote Sri Munshiji's eloquent words again: "Each sculpture has for its main theme the efflorescence of elemental passion, ferocity, death, misery, mobility, power and unsophisticated sexual enjoyment. The panels depict imaginary lions like griffins, elephants running, trotting and jumping, men on running horses, armies marching, *sādhus* preaching, drummers in ridiculous head dresses, their happy mood in tune with the joyous throbbing of the drums, girls dancing in every pose, *nāgas* and *nāginis* (serpent gods and goddesses) standing intertwined and making love and amorous men and women in a variety of poses—all carved in beauty but in naked realism. Everything is mobile, everything expresses the elemental power of the sun."

The erotic sculpture at Konarak, like its counterpart in Khajuraho, has invited a number of ill informed comments from unappreciative foreign critics.

Michael Edwardes (in his book *Indian Temples and Palaces*) sarcastically refers to Konarak as "a **cinema blue** (Blue Film) of the most sophisticated kind."

Zimmer remarks: "Numerous erotic scenes suggest the sensuous delights enjoyed by the happy occupants of the Sun-God's celestial realm, where (to use the language of the tantra) "Bhoga is Yoga", "delight is religion"."

Still others have seen the figures "as representative of objectionable cults associated with the worship of the sun and including orgiastic rites."

The truth lies somewhere else.

In Indian tradition and belief, religion is not something divorced from life. Synthesis of the spiritual and the sensual is a cardinal cornerstone of Indian philosophy.

Long before Sigmund Freud and Havelock Ellis discovered that "*sex is the root of life*", Indian creative genius has recognised the importance of the union of man and woman in creating life, and that one need not be prudish about this vital fact of life.

Even the great recluse philosopher, Sankara, has proclaimed:

Śivaḥ śaktyā yuktó yadi bhavati śaktaḥ prabhavitum,
Na cédévam dévó na khalu kuśalaḥ spanditumapi.

शिवः शक्त्या युक्तो यदि भवति शक्तः प्रभवितुम्।
न चेदेवं देवो न खलु कुशलः स्पन्दितुमपि॥*

"Siva, only when united with his Sakti, is able to create. Otherwise he is not even able to move."

The great prayer, **Lalitatrisati**, refers to the art of love as a facet of the Divine Mother (*Kandarpavidya*).

Hence, let us not be apologetic about the erotic sculpture of Konarak. As Munshiji rightly remarks: "Would it not be better to assume that the masters, who carved these cultural wonders, did not realise that these masterpieces would be looked at by those to whom the beauty of the human body would no longer be divine, to whom the natural would not be admirable, to whom the universal creativeness could not be presented without evoking lewdness?"

As we take leave of the Konarak temple, standing in its lonely majesty, even in its present state of ruins, on the seashore where the waves roar and produce a sound similar to the **Pranava Dhwani** (the primeval sound **AUM**), one feels proud of our great creative genius, which has produced, in Mark Twain's words: **"One of the world's wonders"**, paying tribute to the glory of the vibrant sun, whose eternal temple is the life lived on earth, and whose energy permeates all living beings, vesting them with vitality and procreative power.

---

*Saundaryalahari, verse 1.

XV

Halebid

The Hallmark of Hoysala Art

Halebid literally means "the old house" or "old ruins". It is the present name of the old city of Dvarasamudra, the capital of the Hoysalas. The name "*Hoysala*" is derived from "*Poysala*" which has the meaning "*the striking sala*". The historical founder of the dynasty was a Sala, who struck and killed a tiger with an iron rod at the behest of a sage. This act also furnished the emblem for the dynasty.

The Hoysalas came into prominence in the beginning of the eleventh century A.D. and ruled till 1350. They were earlier the vassals of the Cholas or Chalukyas of Kalyana. In 1045, *Vinayaditya* and his son *Ereyanga* began to assert their power. In 1110-1140 *Bittiga Vishnuvardhana* made the Hoysalas a power to reckon with in South India. He transferred the capital from Velapura (modern Belur) to Dvarasamudra (Halebid).

Vishnuvardhana established his supremacy over a large territory comprising the whole of Mysore and some adjacent areas. His grandson, Viraballala, styled himself *Maharajadhiraja.* His son Viraballala II or Narasimha II lost some territory. The last Hoysala king was Vira Ballala III, who was overcome by Muslim invaders.

Despite their short, fleeting supremacy on the political plane, the Hoysalas were great builders of temples and have bequeathed to us imperishable artistic legacies, at Halebid, Belur and Somnathpur.

We shall first go to Halebid. The starting point is of course the city of Bangalore, which is approachable from all parts of India (and the world) by air or rail.

There is a conducted tour arranged by the tourism department on two days in a week (Thursdays and Sundays) under which you can leave Bangalore at 7 A.M. and return at 1 A.M. after visiting Halebid and Belur and Sravanabelagola. The distances are:

Bangalore to Sravanabelagola	About 65 miles/104 kms
Sravanabelagola to Hassan	About 35 miles/56 kms
Hassan to Belur	About 22 miles/35 kms
Belur to Halebid	About 10 miles/16 kms

Alternatively, one can go from Bangalore to Mysore (a distance of 85 miles/136 kms), seeing the bird sanctuary Ranganathittu and Seringapatna on the way, and stay overnight at Mysore. Next morning we can proceed to Hassan, Belur and Halebid and return to Bangalore by 10 P.M. after seeing Sravanabelagola en-route.

Despite the ravages of history and the passage of time, two temples have remained unscathed at Halebid: *Kedareswara* temple and the *Hoysaleswara* temple, the former being the smaller of the two.

The Kedareswara temple was originally a magnificent temple, star shaped, with 16 points and "filled with sculptures of the very best Indian art". But unfortunately a tree took root in the Vimana (tower) and dislodging the stones reduced it to a heap of ruins, giving the name Halebid or "old ruins" to the place.

The Hoysaleswara temple is a "double" temple, one part dedicated to Siva, the Auspicious One and the other to Sakti, the Divine Mother. The whole temple stands on a terrace five feet six inches in height. It was built in the middle of the 13th century and took 80 years for construction and yet remained incomplete.

One cannot improve upon Fodor's description of this temple. Fodor exclaims: "At Halebid, sculptor's virtuosity reaches its peak—one cannot explain this carving but it is possible to say that these artists were able to treat stone like wood or ivory. One reason, apart from patience and talent, was that they worked in soft soapstone which hardens with time. The friezes are breathtaking: first comes a row of elephants for stability, then one of lordly lions, then above convoluting scrolls of swift horses...mythical beasts and swans follow.

But the largest frieze is also the most exuberant—based on a heavenly theme, it gives heavenly results."

There are 280 carved figures in the Hoysaleswara temple, depicting the various Deities and mythological legends. For example, we have the divine couple, *Siva* and *Parvati* riding the Bull, dancing Siva trouncing the elephant Demon and Nataraja dancing the *Tandava* in unalloyed bliss. There is a fine depiction of the *Varaha episode*,* as also beautiful images of the darling Deity, Ganesha, in various poses.

There are a large number of female figures—in fact, two thirds of the total number—playing the flute, the cymbal or dancing. These figures show "curvacious, heavenly maidens lavishly adorned with gorgeous jewels and posed arrestingly under sculptured awnings."

Carvings in Halebid exist not only in the outer facades, but also in the cool interiors. Opposite the temple there is an open air museum of sculpture, in which there are a number of Ganeshas.

The outstanding feature of the sculptures in Halebid is its ornate nature, reminding Westerners of its similarity with Baroque and Rococo styles of medieval Europe.

As Fergusson remarks: "Here the artistic combination of horizontal with vertical lines and the play of outline and light and shade, far surpass anything in Gothic art. The effects are just what the medieval architects were often aiming at, but which they never attained so perfectly as was done at Halebid."

Fergusson places Halebid temple and the *Parthenon* as two extremes of architectural art, and says: "It would be possible to arrange all the buildings of the world between these two extremes, as they tended towards the severe intellectual purity of the one, or the playful exuberant fancy of the other, but perfection, if it existed, would be somewhere near the mean."

Whatever be the critical comments of the Western experts, Halebid is a feast to the eyes of the Indian visitor and music for his soul. One can never tire seeing the magnificent depictions of the favourite Deities in all their adorned glory.

Hoysala art at Halebid represents a golden mean between Ellora and Khajuraho. The gigantic figures of Ellora are too ethereal,

---

*Vishnu incarnating as a boar to rescue the earth from swirling waters.

too other-worldly and too spiritual, while the diminutive figures of Khajuraho are too fleshy, too sensual and too earthy. The Halebid figures, neither too small nor too big, set in a decorative setting, convey the correct blend of approachable divinity, comprehensible to the common people.

XVI

Belur

Beautiful Ballerinas in Stone

Belur's chief attraction is the *Chennakesava* temple. **Chenna** in Kannada means "beautiful". The Belur temple is dedicated to beautiful Lord Krishna.

Built in the twelfth century, contemporaneous with the famous European Cathedrals, at Chartres and Rheims, it has all the ingredients of Gothic and Baroque art, in architecture and sculpture.

The temple was initially built by Vishnuvardhana (the Yadava ruler) commemorating his victory over the Cholas at Thalakad. The style of building was the *vesara* one, which is the combination of the **Nagara** and **Dravidian** styles. The essential features of this type of temple are:

> A star shaped plan, low elevation, wide extension, elaborate pierced windows, cylindrical polished pillars, elevated basements with richly decorated tiers and embellishment with elaborately-carved, decorative sculpture.

Belur, Somnathpur and Halebid are the typical examples of this style of temple architecture.

The beautiful image of Kesava is believed to have been installed in the **Sanctum Sanctorum** in 1117 A.D.

Though initially built by Vishnuvardhana, the temple underwent additions under his son and grandson.

The gateway of the temple was burnt when the Tughlaks under Ganga Salar laid siege to it. The seven-storied *Gopuram*,* which

*Temple tower.

is seen today, was built in 1397 A.D. under the patronage of Vijayanagar rulers.

Minor additions were also made by the chiefs located in Belur, under the sovereignty of the Nayak rulers.

The above historical backdrop explains the existence at Belur of a variety of sculptural styles. Though predominantly Hoysala, there are a number of sculptural pieces characteristic of the Vijayanagar and Nayak periods.

What specially marks the Belur temple is not its architecture, nor the exterior friezes in the typical Hoysala style, which one also sees at the Halebid temples, but the 42 bracket figures of women, of which 38 support the lofts of the temple outside and four crown the pillars inside.

Not very big in size, but exquisitely carved, with a high degree of polish and finesse, these figures—the Indian sculptor's tribute to ideal womanhood: healthy, vibrant and sensuous—virtually represent a beauty parade of Ballerinas. In Fodor's words: "Most of them are voluptuous, full-breasted and full-hipped women, beautifully adorned, and taking any number of graceful poses beneath intricate pierced, scrolled and scalloped stone canopies."

The 42 figures include: the lady with the mirror, the lady with the parrot, the lady in various stages of toilet, the huntress, the lady in various gracious dance poses, the lady playing the flute, the musician, the lady in a man's disguise, the lady with the scorpion, the gypsy girl etc.

The interior of the Belur temple contains exquisitely carved pillars, and some fine specimens of sculpture.

Of these, special mention must be made of **Mohini** which is a fine description of the **Padmini** type of woman (the most superlative among the four types into which women were classified in ancient India, viz., *Padmini, Chitrini, Shankhini* and *Hastini*).

Equally attractive are the majestic **Dwarapalas,*** holding the mace, the discus, the conch and the lotus. The **Narasimha pillar** (which was once a revolving pillar) and the richly carved ceiling of the central hall also arrest attention. These represent in a way the acme of Dravidian sculpture.

---

*Door-keepers.

The Hoysala artist's treatment of animals in sculpture is superb, a crowning example of which is the panel of elephants on the outer walls of the Belur temple. One almost feels the movement of the elephants in procession.

Another outstanding piece of sculpture, not to be missed at Belur, is that of Krishna playing the flute which depicts the Lord lost in the melody of music, while the cows and the herds listen hypnotised.

The Garuda in front of the temple is also a good piece of workmanship.

By the side of the main temple are small shrines: one, the *Channingaraya* temple (supposed to be built by Queen Shantala Devi, wife of Vishnuvardhana) and the other, *Veeranarayana* temple, the sculpture in which resembles that of the Kedareswara temple at Halebid.

Western art critics refer to the plastic exuberance at Belur and bring in comparison with Baroque, Rococo and Gothic art. Great connoisseurs of Indian art, like Ananda Coomaraswamy, have paid tribute to the temple architecture of Belur as a synthesis of the Nagara and Dravidian styles of temple building.

But what lingers in the mind of the ordinary visitor to Belur is the tribute which the sculptor has paid, with his chisel and hammer, to Indian womanhood—nay to all womankind: their grace, charm and captivating sensuousness.

A garrulous tourist guide once mentioned to me that all Indian sculpture is based on two ancient works: "the *Kamasutra* and the *Natyasastra*". I did not take him seriously. But after a visit to Khajuraho and Belur one feels that there might be an element of truth in the zealous guide's assertion.

The Belur sculptor had probably the *Natyasastra* in mind while carving out the various *Madanikas.**

Here woman is depicted in her own pristine glory, without the interfering presence of the dominating male.

What, in essence, the Belur sculptor has done is to pay homage to the Supreme Sakti whose facets on earth women are:

---

*"Madanikas" means courtesans.

Vidyā Samastāḥ Tava Devi Bhedāḥ
Striyaḥ Samastā Sakalā Jagatsu.

One remembers the hymn from the **Devimahatmya**, as one reluctantly takes leave of the beautiful ballerinas of Belur.

XVII

Khajuraho

The Silver-laden City of the Chandellas

As I was planning a road journey from Delhi to Madras, a friend advised that by making slight detours, I could include in my itinerary the Khajuraho temples of Madhya Pradesh and the caves of Ajanta and Ellora in Maharashtra. I gladly accepted the advice.

The first day's journey took us from Delhi to Chattarpur via Agra, Gwalior and Jhansi—a total distance of 340 miles. We halted for a night at Chattarpur with a friend and started early morning for Khajuraho which was about 30 miles away. The drive to Khajuraho through lush vegetation was very pleasant and we reached Khajuraho at about ten in the morning.

There are, of course, other ways to get to Khajuraho. One can fly by a daily Indian Airlines flight from Delhi, Agra or Varanasi. If one travels by rail (from Madras to Delhi) one can get down at Jhansi (from Calcutta or Bombay), at *Satna* or *Harpalpur.* Khajuraho is 110 miles from Jhansi, 80 miles from Satna and 66 miles from Harpalpur, by road.

What does the word "**Khajuraho**" mean? It is a distortion of the Sanskrit word "**Kharj-urav-ahaka**". "**Kharj-ura**" in Sanskrit means the date-tree as also silver. Though one can still see an old date palm or two in Khajuraho, I would prefer the meaning silver and call Khajuraho "The Silver-laden City of the Chandellas", symbolising their prosperity and power.

Who were the Chandellas? Browsing through the History book, one finds that they were the local vassals of the Imperial **Pratiharas** who gained ascendance in North India, after the disintegration of Harshavardhana's empire in the middle of the seventh century A.D.

The first Chandella prince, who asserted his independence, was **Yasovarman**, who, in 940 A.D., retrieved the fort of **Kalanjara** from the Rashtrakutas and retained it for himself.

Yasovarman built the first temple in Khajuraho, the *Lakshmana* temple in 954 A.D. He was succeeded by his son **Dhanga** (who ruled between 960 and 1002 A.D.) who built the two temples of *Viswanatha* and *Parsvanatha.*

Dhanga's son, **Ganda** (who ruled between 1002 and 1017 A.D.), built the *Devi Jagadamba* and *Chitragupta* temples. Ganda's successor was his son **Vidyadhara** who ruled from 1017 A.D. to 1029 A.D. Vidyadhara was the most powerful Chandella ruler and he built the *Kandariya Mahadeva* temple, which is the largest and the most beautiful of the temples of Khajuraho.

After Vidyadhara, Chandella power declined. Though temples were continued to be built till 1335 A.D., the main temples, eighty-five in number, were built between 950 A.D. and 1050 A.D. Of these barely twenty remain. The lapse of long centuries has worked havoc on the rest of them.

The Khajuraho temples, with their upward surging **Sikharas**,* are located in three groups. The western group comprises mainly the famous Kandariya Mahadeva temple, Devi Jagadamba temple, Lakshmana temple, Viswanatha and Nandi temples.

The eastern group consists of three Hindu temples and three Jain temples, the largest and finest of these is the Parsvanatha temple.

The southern group, not as important as the other two, comprises the **Dulhadeva** and **Chaturbhuj** temples.

The building material used in these temples is sandstone. All the shrines abound in sumptuous sculptures. The skilled sculptors have carved beautiful images of lovers in embrace, gods and goddesses in various poses, attractive *Madanikas* in various stages of

*Spires.

toilet, elephants and horses in playful moods, leogriffs and gryphons galore.

The carvings of the beautifully shaped men and women and the vibrant animals are exquisite and display craftsmanship of a high order.

The artists and artisans who carved these splendid images must have drawn their models from life and one feels proud that in India, the male and female forms existed in such enviable shapes—a lie to the other-worldly attitude levelled against Indians by the West and a positive indication that **joie de vivre** was not absent in India even a thousand years ago.

Much has been written about the erotic sculpture in the temples of Khajuraho by western critics. Even experts, like Hermann Goetze, consider the great temples of Khajuraho "an anomaly" and as "shrines erected for a depraved sect held in contempt by most cultured people of that time" meaning thereby that the Tantric sects like the **Kaula** Kapalikas, to whose heresies, according to him, the Chandella Rulers like Dhanga and Ganda are deemed to have succumbed and produced the sculpture of **Maithuna*** figures in Khajuraho!

While respecting the erudition of such experts, one has to disagree with such a lopsided view. As Hugh and Colleen Gantzer pointed out (in the *Indian Express* dated February 16, 1980), the erotic depictions "are neither predominant nor embarrassingly obtrusive. They are as much or as little a part of the entire rich profusion of detailed carvings as are the scenes of war, worship, music, dance, daily living and mythology. Horses prance in battle, mendicants pray, musicians flute pipes, clash cymbals, rumble drums, dancers sway lissomly, couples gaze in secret rapture and gods and griffons rear in terrifying protection."

The sculptures in Khajuraho are not an aberration or an anomaly. They represent (as the temple sculptures elsewhere do) the finest expression of the genius of India which does not believe in divorcing religion from life, but affirms its faith in the synthesis of the sensual with the spiritual.

The Khajuraho sculptures, viewed in isolation, can be deemed as a tribute to the glory of the flesh.

---

*Maithuna figures are loving couples in union.

But the more appropriate assessment would to see them in their correct juxtaposition in relation to the soaring spires of the shrines, which the Chandella Rulers built as monuments to the Supreme Spirit, in pious devotion.

XVIII

Suchindram

The Sanctuary of Sthanunatha*

Suchindram is a small village located between Nagercoil and Kanyakumari, four miles from the former and six miles from the latter.

Why the name Suchindram? **Suchitah Indrah atra iti Suchindram**: it is the place where Indra got purified.

The story of Indra and Ahalya is too well known to need lengthy narration. Rajaji's version of it in his condensation of "*Ramayana*" cannot be improved upon:

"Sage Gautama lived with his wife Ahalya, spending his days in peace and holy meditation. One day during the sage's absence from Ashrama, Indra filled with unholy desire for the beautiful Ahalya entered it, disguised as Gautama and approached the lady with urgent solicitation. She was not deceived by the impersonation, but vain of her beauty and proud that it had won her the love of the Lord of the Celestials, she lost her judgment and yielded to his desire.

"When the sin had been sinned, realising its heinousness and the fierce spiritual energy of her betrayed husband, she warned Indra of his terrible peril and begged him to be gone in the instant.

"Indra was fleeing in guilty panic, but unfortunately for him, he almost bumped into the *rishi* who was just returning from his

*Sthanunatha means The Permanent One.

ablutions, clad in wet garments, and radiating spiritual lustre. Pretence was hopeless before the all-seeing wisdom and Indra bowed in abject supplication and threw himself on the mercy of the rishi. The sage looked at him with wrath and loathing and cursed him: "Lustful beast as you are, dead to all truth and righteousness, may your manhood fall away from you." Indra at once became a eunuch and went back to the *Devas* in ignominious shame."

For a long time he did penance to expiate his sin. The merciful Lord Siva, the Auspicious One, took pity on him and purified him. The place where Indra did his penance was called *Jnānāranya.* It was renamed Suchindram after the purification of Indra.

The Suchindram temple is believed to have been built by Indra, who is deemed to worship every night even today at the shrine.

The legend of Indra's purification is only one part of the story of the Suchindram temple. The other is the one relating to the chastity of Anasuya.

Sage Atri and his devoted wife Anasuya stayed at Jnanaranya. Anasuya's devotion to her husband was proverbial and the three deities, *Brahma, Vishnu* and *Siva,* wanted the whole world to know of it, across the barriers of time and space. They appeared as begging Brahmins before her and when she was about to serve them food, imposed a condition that they would eat only if she served in the nude. The chaste Anasuya converted through the power of her chastity the three gods into three babies and suckled them.

Atri returned, and on the supplication of the Goddesses, Saraswati, Lakshmi and Parvati, and of sages and angels, Anasuya restored the deities to their original glory. They, along with their spouses, blessed the holy couple and disappeared. On the very spot sprouted three lingas under an Amaltas tree which exists to this day.

Atri and Anasuya offered worship at the shrine, which is now famous as the Suchindram temple.

It is thus in essence a Trinity temple, though the main *sanctum sanctorum* is dedicated to *Sthanunatha,* Siva as the Eternal, Permanent One, who is ever waiting to wed his beloved, who remains, garland in hand, a few miles away at Kanyakumari, their mythical marriage in a particular incarnation having been thwarted by the machinations of Narada.

So much for the myth and legend connected with Suchindram.

Now a little of history. Researches conducted on parts of the Amaltas tree show that the tree is 2000 years old. Some parts of the present temple were built before 947 A.D. and some before the 12th century. The Pandya, Chera and Chola rulers have added substantially to the temple during the fifteenth and nineteenth centuries.

Tirumalai Nayakar gave the finishing touches by building the shrine for Garuda.

The sculptural feast at the Suchindram temple is so sumptuous that one does not know where to begin description and where to end.

The temple tower (*Gopuram*) is 134 feet high and stands out majestically against the sky, amidst green coconut trees and by the side of the temple tank.

The main areas of the temple, sculptured and pillared with exquisite carvings, are: The *Nātakasala*; the *Unjal Mandapam*; the Lengthy Corridors (the Suchindram corridor is second in length only to the Rameshwaram corridor, but the granite pillars with the sculptured ladies with the lamps make it more beautiful than Rameshwaram); the *Ganesha* and *Muruga* shrines; the *Alankara Mandapam* which contains the famous musical pillars; the Devi shrine; the *Hanuman* Mandir; the *Chitra* Sabha; the Shrine of *Vishnu*; the sanctum of *Konnayadi*, where the three lingas sprouted under the Amaltas tree; the *Garuda Mandapam* and the *Chempakaraman Mandapam*, a beautiful pavilion with 32 sculptural pillars, depicting legends linked to the deities in the temple.

The *sanctum sanctorum* contains the idol of Siva, the Linga and opposite stands the dutiful Nandi,* 12.5 feet in height and a sculptural masterpiece.

By the side of the *sanctum sanctorum* is the shrine of Vishnu where all the forms of worship conducted at the sanctum sanctorum are simultaneously done, proclaiming the essential oneness of the two deities, *Vishnu* and *Siva*.

On the northern side of the *sanctum sanctorum* is the shrine of *Nataraja*, the eternal dancer.

---

*Siva's bull.

There is a shrine in honour of the nine planets, *Navagrahas,* called the *Vasanta Mandapam.* Unlike in other temples, the images of the Navagrahas have been carved on the ceiling so that one has to look up to bow in veneration.

There is a pretty little shrine in honour of Sita and Rama at the northern end of the western corridor and right opposite at the other end stands the gigantic *Hanuman,* a figure 18 feet in height, depicting the *Viswarūpadarsana* given to Sita in the Asoka forest. It is an awe-inspiring vision and we mentally acknowledge our gratitude to the anonymous sculptor who created it.

We can go on describing the various facets of the temple, rich in artistic creation, rich in mythological tradition, rich in its spiritual and moral meaning to an erring effete humanity.

A visit to the Suchindram temple is rewarding in many ways. The artistic connoisseur and the discerning archaeologist can spend hours and days, enjoying the mix of Dravidian styles of art and architecture presented, bequeathed by the Pandyan, Chera and Chola dynasties.

The religious worshipper can enjoy the traditional forms of worship, continued to this day in an unbroken tradition, derived from hoary sources of mythology and legend.

Suchindram temple, a temple to the Hindu Trinity of Vishnu, Siva and Brahma: *Sthanu, Mal* and *Aya* (Sthanumalaya) as they are locally called, is a lesson in monument to the Vaishnava and Saivite religious factions, who, to this day, see only the differences and hesitate even to intermarry.

It is a noble reminder to the ideals of chastity, symbolised by *Anasuya,* a precious heritage of Indian womanhood.

Lastly, being the place where even the errant Indra was purified, Suchindram teaches us that though, driven by our animal passions and disturbed minds, we commit sin and invite suffering, there is a way to overcome our weaknesses and lead a life of purity and happiness, harmony and peace, by worshipping an eternal Trinity, residing within ourselves.

XIX

Mandu

Myths and Memories of Malwa

There is a popular saying that the mornings of *Varanasi*, the evenings of *Oudh* (present-day Lucknow) and the nights of *Malwa* are inimitable. One realises the truth of this when one spends a moonlit night at one of the *mahals* of Mandu, a city now in ruins, but which, once upon a time, was the flourishing capital of Malwa land.

Mandu is a distortion of the word *Mandav* or *Mandap* which was the military capital of Bhoja Raja who ruled in the eleventh century (between 1010 and 1055 A.D.). Bhoja had three capitals, *Ujjain*, the political capital, *Mandap*, the military capital and *Dhar*, the family capital.

The Mandu fort is the biggest fort in the world, with a circumference of 40 miles. It is 4000 years old.

Malwa was ruled by several successive dynasties and Mandu served every one of them as a military base: First the *Mauryas*, then the *Sakas* and later *Harsha*, the *Rajputs*, *Bhoja*, the *Parmars* and finally, the Muslim rulers: the *Ghoris*, the *Khiljis* and the *Mughals* whose impress survives even to this day. The last Khilji ruler, Sultan Baz Bahadur, was the son of Sher Shah's general. Akbar defeated him at the battle of Shajapur and Malwa came under the Mughals. After the decline of the Mughals, Mandu came under the Pawar rulers of Dhar state.

Mandu was once a prosperous city with a population of 5,00,000. It had 60 lakes and 700 temples within the fort area. Its location is at the centre of India so that rivers on one side flow into the Bay of Bengal and rivers on the other side flow into the Arabian Sea.

Mandu is about 60 miles from Indore by road. Any amount of description cannot capture the magical charm of Mandu, which has to be seen and enjoyed.

As the Madhya Pradesh Tourism Development Corporation eloquently proclaims: "Mandu is memories based in history, its solitude caressed by the soothing Malwa breeze...Beautiful Mandu. Wondrous Mandu. Incredible Mandu. A city silent and waiting. A city built for joy and laughter and music...Mandu that once was *Shadiabad*, "*The Citadel of Joy*", where the rulers of Malwa revelled in pleasure and luxury...recalling a time when the Afghans marched in and crafted its Mahals standing with the dignity of Romanesque cathedrals, colonnades and arches with forested symmetry, and cleverly fashioned domes that echo even a whisper from one distant end to the other. A vast symphony of palaces, lakes and lush green."

Mandu stands today a deserted city, sprawled across a vast plateau, perched on the end of the Vindhya Mountains.

The main monuments to be seen at Mandu can be divided into three groups:

The Village Group,
The Royal Enclave, and
Rewa Kund Group.

It is better to start our visit with the village group, where the real history of Mandu begins. This group contains the following monuments:

Taveli Mahal,
Delhi Gate,
Great Mosque, and
Ashrafi Mahal.

Hoshang Shah, son of Dilawar Khan, the rebellious governor of Muhammed Bin Tughlak, was the first ruler of the Ghori dynasty, who, in 1405, shifted the capital to Mandu and started building in a big way. All the monuments in the village group are the creations of Hoshang Shah. His own tomb started by him was completed by his son and successor.

Hoshang Shah's tomb, in white marble, is one of the outstanding relics in Mandu. It is said that Shah Jahan was so much impressed with Hoshang's tomb that he sent architects to study it before undertaking the Taj Mahal.

The Great Mosque of Jama Masjid, though fashioned after the great mosque of Damascus, is no mere imitation and is considered a fine example of Afghan Architecture in India.

The Ashrafi Mahal, originally built as a school by Hoshang's nephew, Mahmud Shah, finally became his tomb.

The main sights of the Royal Enclave are: *Jahaj Mahal, Hindola Mahal* and *Champa Baoli.*

The *Jahaj Mahal* or the ship palace was built by Ghiasud Din for his harem. As Fodor observes: "By moonlight, this haunting palace reflected in the lakes almost looks as though it might slip into the waters for some nocturnal journey."

The *Hindola Mahal* or the swinging palace, built as a Royal Audience Hall, has inwardly sloping halls which convey the disquieting impression that the whole solid mass is swaying.

The *Champa Baoli* is a well with fragrant water, used for air-conditioning the rooms.

The Rewa Kund Group contains the *Hathi Mahal* or the Elephant Palace, Chistikhan's Palace, Nilkanth, a palace with a pool in the country yard, watered by a cascade running through one of the rooms, and most important of all, the *Rupmati* pavilion and the *Baz Bahadur* pavilion.

The legend of love between Baz Bahadur and Rupmati is an immortal romance enshrined in the memories of Malwa through its folk songs.

Baz Bahadur was the last independent ruler of Mandu. Fond of music, he fell in love with a beautiful, tribal singer called Rupmati who lived on the banks of the Narmada river. He brought her to Mandu to live with him. They spent beautiful days together in music and love. He built a high pavilion for her so that she could see the distant river at sunset.

Their love story met with a tragic end, when Baz Bahadur was defeated and killed by Adham Khan, Akbar's General and Rupmati committed suicide before she could be captured by the lustful general.

A visit to Mandu gives one nostalgic memories of the romantic past—a past in which there was valour and war, as also love and fidelity.

As Hugh and Colleen Gantzer beautifully sum up their impressions of Mandu:

"...A fortress which was won with austerity and valour, crafted with strength and skill and love, faded out of history with songs and a suicide.

"And now, only the monuments and memories remain in the high and brooding moon-touched vastness of Mandu."

XX

Madurai

Majestic Monument to Mellifluous Meenakshi

Madurai (literally, the Sweet Place), "The Beating Heart of the Land of the Tamils" as Fodor calls it, is a hoary city more than 3000 years old.

From the earliest times, it was the capital of the Pandya rulers and the seat of *Sangam*, the Tamil Academy which sat in judgement on Tamil literary works. It is also the city, once burnt by the anger of the chaste Kannagi, when a Pandyan ruler, in an erroneous judgement, sentenced her husband Kovalan to death.

But it is the Meenakshi temple which has sustained the city through the vicissitudes of history, located at the centre in an area of fifteen acres, that is the life and soul of the city. The temple and the city, built simultaneously, have grown feeding each other.

The earliest known Pandyan ruler was *Kulasekhara*, who is reported to have built the Meenakshi temple, 3006 years ago. Additions and alterations were made by subsequent rulers and the massive finishing contributions were made by Tirumala Nayak.

The bulk of the sculpture that we see today in Madurai temple belongs to the Nayak period. The Nayaks ruled Madurai between 1560 and 1743 A.D., the first Nayak ruler being *Visvanatha*, a Vijayanagar Viceroy.

There are legends galore linking Madurai with the Great God Siva, the Auspicious One, who is stated to have performed here his sixty-four *Leelas.** But the most important legend is the one of His marriage to *Meenakshi,* who was born as a Pandyan princess, the daughter of Pandyan King **Malayadhwaja**.

This important event has been immortalised in a famous sculpture in the Meenakshi temple. The coy bride is shown as being given in marriage by Vishnu, her brother, to Siva, the bridegroom. It is a masterpiece, rarely rivalled in artistic composition, craftsmanship and devotional spirit.

The **marriage of Meenakshi** to Siva is considered by Zimmer as symbolic of Aryan and Dravidian religious cults. It is also symbolic of the synthesis of Vaishnava and Saivite sects.

A foreign tourist expressed his surprise over the lack of intermarriages between Vaishnavites and Saivites in South India, even today, when the classic example of Meenakshi's marriage to Siva was so strikingly displayed before them.

Meenakshi is the unifying link: the sister of Vishnu and the spouse of Siva! The sage of Kanchi drove home this point of unity in a number of articles in a Tamil Journal under the title *Sivathin Sakti, Narayana Sodari* (Sakti of Siva, Sister of Vishnu), but the message has not still moved the majority.

The emerald-hued black stone image of Meenakshi in the **Sanctum Sanctorum** is a captivating vision, created by the skill and devotion of the unknown sculptor who has concretised Divinity, in peerless grace.

There are twelve *Gopurams* in the temple, the largest of them being the Southern one which is 160 feet high and was built in 1559. The oldest Gopuram is the Eastern one, built by Maravarman Sundara Pandyan in 1216-1238 A.D.

At Madurai, one first visits the sanctuary of the Mother before going to pay obeisance to the Father. En-route is the gigantic image of Ganesha or Vinayaka. He is called **Mukkurni** Vinayaka, since he likes and is given an offering of rice cake made of three **Kurnis** (a kind of measure).

There are a number of *Mandapams* in the Meenakshi temple, each one containing a veritable feast of sculpture.

First there is the **Kambatti Mandapam**, in which various

---

*"Leelas" means "sports".

manifestations of Siva have been carved out. The famous sculpture, "*Marriage of Meenakshi*", is also in this Mandapam.

The other Mandapams are the **Ashtasakti** Mandapa, containing the sculptures of Eight Saktis, the *Puthu Mandapa* (the New Mandapa) constructed by Tirumala Nayak, containing a large number of exquisite sculpture pieces, and the thousand-pillared Mandapa, which has now been converted into an Art Gallery and Museum.

Though it is called the Hall of Thousand Pillars, it has only 997 pillars. It was built in 1560 A.D. and is a structure where the engineering skill and artistic vision have blended beautifully.

Each pillar contains a carved figure. The more prominent among the carved figures are those of *Rati* (wife of Cupid), *Kartikeya, Ganesha, Siva* as the wandering mendicant and endless number of *Yālis,* which are mythical figures of Giant Lions.

Outside the Hall of Thousand Pillars are the famous musical pillars, which, when struck, produce musical notes.

There is a special figure of Nataraja in the Madurai temple which differs radically from the usual Chola Bronzes, in one important detail: in the usual Chola images the Lord is shown as dancing with the left leg raised, but in Madurai, he is dancing with the right leg raised.

This reversal of leg (called **Marukal** in Tamil) is linked with a legend. Pandya King, Rajasekhara, who felt worried about the strain that would be caused to the Lord by always dancing with the left leg raised is said to have requested the Lord to change the legs to relieve the strain and got a graceful acquiescence from the Divine Master.

In front of the Meenakshi sanctorum is the famous Lily tank, which was used in the Sangam days to test the quality of literary works. The manuscript was placed on the water of the tank, deserving works floated and did not sink down. Thiruvalluvar's **Kural** was one such work.

Though Madurai was the Pandyan Capital, much of present-day Madurai we see is the impress of Nayak Rule, especially of Tirumalai Nayak, who was a contemporary of Shah Jahan.

Apart from a few Gopurams, the *Puthumandapam* and several sculptural pieces which adorn the Meenakshi temple, Tirumala Nayak built his palace nearby, which is a building in which a synthesis of several architectural styles has been attempted, especially Indian and Saracen.

After a visit to Madurai, what lingers on in the memory is not the tall Gopurams of the temple—very few other temples in India have such a large number of towering Gopurams—not the profusion of beautiful sculpture in which the zenith of Dravidian art finds expression, not The Hall of Thousand Pillars—which Fergusson called "**The Wonder of the Place**" and the sculptures which, according to him, "surpassed those of any other hall I have seen", not the massive golden lily tank with its mythical reputation and legendary links with celestial beings, but the beautiful image of Meenakshi, the fish-eyed goddess herself: majestic, alluring, compassionate, oozing sweetness, seeing whom the great Carnatic composer Muthuswami Dikshitar burst into a musical composition, the English rendering of which is as under:

"O! Meenakshi!" Fish-eyed Goddess! Grant me bliss!
O! Passionate one! Daughter of the King!
O! Illusory one!
O! Emerald-hued one! O! Siva's spouse!
O! Blue-eyed one! Who liberates from earthly bonds!
O! Proud one! Who lives in the ***Kadamba*** *forest!*
O! Resident of Madurai! encircled by Gems!
O! Daughter of King Malayadhwaja Pandya!
O! Moon-faced one! O! Victorious one!
O! Kind one! Who creates ten nuances of music from the veena!
O! Beloved of the Great God Sundareswara!
Sister of Vishnu, the enemy of Madhu and Mura,
O! Slender-waisted one!
O! Auspicious One! Grant me bliss.

XXI

Chittor

Courage and Chivalry

Few monuments evoke the same emotional turmoil as the ruins of Chittor fort which lies 72 miles east of Udaipur.

Chittor was the capital of Mewar where honour was prized above safety, chastity held dearer than life. Bappa Rawal, Rana Pratap, Rani Padmini, Rana Kumbha, Rana Sanga and the immortal Mira are among the names that spring to memory.

Chittor derives its name from its founder, Chitrang, the Mori prince of the Parmar family, which ruled Malwa as part of Hindustan. Chittor is a distortion of the word '*Chitrakot*'.

In 734 A.D. Bappa Rawal took the fort of Chittor from Moun Mori and founded the Guhilot dynasty in Mewar. From 734 to 1567 Chittor remained the capital of Mewar and 59 princes sat on the throne of Chittor.

The fort was sacked thrice: first by Alauddin Khilji in 1303 A.D., second time by Bahadur Shah of Gujarat in 1534 A.D. and the third time by Akbar in 1567 A.D.

Each sack resulted in plunder and arson. In the words of Annie Besant: "Chittor is one of the cities that seemed to have been doomed to continual struggle and gateway after gateway on the ascent is marked with stones that tell how a hero fought and died. She sits on her mountain-top, though discrowned, and gazes over the plains that she has often seen glittering with lance points, quivering under the hoop of charging squadrons."

About the first sack by Alauddin Khilji, Fodor writes: "This has been likened to a second Troy since the cause of the trouble was the desire of the Moslem ruler to secure the hand of Rani Padmini, the Indian Helen said to be the most beautiful woman in the world. As the city tottered to its fall by the onslaught, a funeral pyre was kindled in a vault. Into it plunged the Rajput women, singing as they went, gaily decked out in their bridal robes. In the royal fashion, Padmini herself brought up the rear of this procession of death...all that the conqueror found on entering the city was a wisp of smoke gently ascending from the silent vault."

In the second siege by Sultan Bahadur Shah, 32,000 Rajputs died in battle and 13,000 women by "*Jauhar*" (Self-immolation).

In the third siege, Akbar was so deeply impressed by the heroism of the two defending Rajput commanders, Jaimal and Patta (celebrated in several Rajput ballads) that he erected two statues on elephants in their memory and had them set up at the entrance to his palace at Agra.

After the fall of Chittor, the Sisodia capital was shifted to Udaipur.

Chittor fort is at a height of 500 feet above the town, which itself is located at 1350 feet above sea level. Its circumference at the base is eight miles. The zig-zag ascent to the fort is guarded by seven gateways by guard-rooms.

The most outstanding monument inside the fort is the *Tower of Victory* built by Rana Kumbha in 1448 to commemorate his victory over the Muslim kings of Gujarat and Malwa. The tower is 122 feet in height and was built in eight years. Sculpture depicting scenes from Hindu mythology and the Hindu pantheon of deities covers the entire surface, but this does not in any way detract from the monumental outline of the tower.

The other remains include the palaces of *Jaimal* and *Patta* and *Bhim Singh*, the palaces of Rana Kumbha and of Padmini and many Hindu and Jain temples, the most prominent being the *Kalikamata* temple and the temple of *Mirabai*.

Mira was born in 1504. She was married to Prince Bhoja Raj, the eldest son of Rana Sanga of Chittor. Her God-intoxication posed problems for her husband, father and father-in-law, all of whom died before Mira attained the age of 24. Subjected to many hardships by Prince Bikramjeet, Mira left Chittor and first went to Merta, her birth-place and later went to Dwaraka, where she died in 1546 at the age of 43.

Chittor was thus sanctified not only by the blood and tears of Rajput chivalry and chastity but also by the travails of Mira, the mystic poet lover of God.

Rana Pratap, the indomitable Rajput warrior, tried his best to recover Chittor, but he could not succeed.

"To commemorate the desolation of Chittor, he interdicted to himself and his successors every article of luxury and pomp, until the insignia of her glory should be received. The gold and silver dishes were laid aside for 'pattras' of leaves, their beds henceforth of straw and their beards left untouched."

The mere mention of Rana Pratap's name stirs pride and patriotism in every Indian's heart. Though he failed to take back the fort from the formidable Akbar, Rana Pratap never bowed his head and preserved the honour of his race. In a way, Chittor represents the spirit of Rana Pratap. To borrow the words of Tod of the '*Annals of Rajasthan*':

"Undaunted heroism, inflexible fortitude, that which keeps honour bright, perseverance with fidelity such as no nation can boast were the materials opposed to soaring ambition, commanding talents, unlimited means and the fervour of religious zeal."

We feel proud that we are the inheritors of a spirit that defied defeat with death, that hardly 500 years ago, we had brave men who held country above their petty selves and women who were symbols of chastity and preferred destruction to dishonour.

Standing on the ramparts of the fort one recalls Vivekananda's words: "When you have men who are ready to sacrifice their everything for their country, sincere to the backbone, when such men arise, India will become great in every respect."

XXII

Mount Abu

The Mansion of Marble Magic

The Dilwara temples of Mount Abu have won superlative encomia from esteemed Englishmen. Tod, the author of "*The Annals of Rajasthan*", wrote: "This is the most superb of all temples of India, and there is not an edifice besides the Taj that can approach it."

Sir Edwin Arnold considered that such workmanship was possible of achievement only with the aid of Alladin's wonderful lamp.

Henry Cousens, in his book "*Architectural Antiquities of Western India*", observed: "The crisp, thin, translucent, shell-like treatment of the marble surpasses anything seen elsewhere and some of the designs are veritable dreams of beauty."

According to Fodor, the exuberance of sculpture at the Dilwara temples attains the zenith of Indian inventive genius in the art of decoration.

What else is required besides the words of three experts to rouse one's curiosity and propel one to proceed to Mount Abu, often described by zealous tourist guides as the "Olympus of Rajasthan"?

Mount Abu a tiny hill station with an altitude of 4000 feet above sea level is located at a distance of 20 miles from Abu Road Railway Station, on the Delhi-Ahmedabad rail route. The train travel time to reach Abu Road station is 18 hours from Delhi, 16 from

Bombay and five from Ahmedabad, the mileage covered being 480 miles from Delhi, 423 miles from Bombay and 116 miles from Ahmedabad.

The term Abu is derived from **Arbuda**, the mythological son of Himalayas, who was supposed to have saved Nandi, the sacred bull of Siva from a pit into which it had fallen.

Abu is also considered the hermitage of the epic Sage **Vasishta**. But these mythological links better be lost in the mists of memory.

We are going to Mount Abu to see the marvellous Jain temples, five in number but only two are world famous: the ones built by *Vimal Shah* and *Tejpal* in 1031 and 1230 A.D.

Who were these gentlemen who built these enchanting temples and how did they come to build them? How did Jainism come to Abu? What is the historical backdrop to these fascinating questions and their answers?

Heinrich Zimmer, in his monumental work "*The Art of Indian Asia*", writes: "The chief period of Jaina temple building began within seven years of the Mohammedan sack of Somnath by Mahmud of Ghazni in 1024 and ended within a few years of the invasion of Gujarat by Allaudin Khilji in 1297.

"The aspirations and the dynamic consciousness of a great era of Indian national life thus were crystallised in this richly flowering architecture. It was a brief but a glorious day, burning with the fine frenzy of the religious zeal that flared in reply to the iconoclastic ruthlessness of the Muslim invaders.

"The temple of Somnath, the fabulous magnificence of which has never since been surpassed, had been outrageously desecrated and destroyed by Mahmud. His act of barbarism intensified among the native Indians an activity that had already begun, even prior to the invasion and during the few years that remained before the fall of northern India, buildings rose multitudinously in living protest. Moreover, by this time patronage had passed into the hands of the merchants and humbler subjects, so that the temples of Mount Abu can be regarded as an architecture of the people, as distinguished from the architecture of the kings."

One may or may not agree with Zimmer's views. But his remarks offer an explanation as to why, though Jainism is a religion which does not believe in a God or incarnations of a God nor in idol worship, the temples of Mount Abu are a riot of sumptuous sculpture, of gods and goddesses, and incarnations, chiselled majestically out of marble.

Will Durant considers the temples of *Vimal* and *Tejpal* as the greatest achievement of Jains in the field of art. To quote him: "The dome of the Tejpala shrine is one of those overwhelming experiences which doom all writing about art to impotence and futility. The temple of Vimala, built entirely of white marble, is a maze of irregular pillars joined with fanciful brackets to a more simple carved entablature; above is a marble dome too opulent in statuary, but carved into a stone lacework of moving magnificence", "finished", says Fergusson, "with a delicacy of detail and appropriateness of ornament which is probably unsurpassed by any similar example to be found anywhere else. Those introduced by the architects in Henry VII's chapel at Westminster or at Oxford, are coarse and clumsy in comparison."

Vimal Shah was a minister at the court of Bhim Deva, the first Solanki ruler of Gujarat. The Vimal Vasahi temple, which he built, was started in 1031 and was completed in 14 years. 1200 workers laboured on it. It is dedicated to Adinath, the first Jain Tirthankara. According to the Jains "their faith is eternal and has been revealed through the successive ages of the world by the *Tirthankaras,* a line of saints or prophets, 24 in number, each of whom attained perfection and absolute freedom and then preached Jainism to the world."

Though Vimal Shah was a devout Jain, his family deity was *Ambaji,* the Divine Mother and this probably explains the importance given to the depiction of the 16 manifestations of Sakti (*Vidya Devis*) in the supporting pillars of the marble dome.

Tejpal who built the later temple in 1231 and dedicated it to the 22nd Tirthankara, *Neminath,* was minister to Rama Vir Dhaval. He is said to have built the temple with the help of his brother Vastupal at the specific insistence of his wife *Annapurna.*

The most striking feature of the Tejpal temple is the marble pendant of the temple dome which, as Fergusson put it, "hangs from the centre more like a cluster of crystal drops than a solid mass of marble."

The marble with which both the temples were built was quarried in the plains below and carted 4000 feet up.

While admiring the breathtaking beauty of the delicate marble carvings in the Jain temples of Mount Abu, certain critics have observed that these represent a "frozen lifeless beauty devoid of true monumentality". In fact, such criticism has been extended to all Indian sculpture by even experts like Will Durant with the remark that "the sculpture of India never acquired the grace of her literature, or the sublimity of her architecture, or the depth of her philosophy; it mirrored chiefly the confused and uncertain spirit of her religions."

One has to respectfully disagree with such views. The creative genius of India has found its untrammelled outpouring in marble and sandstone, granite and bronze and attained the zenith of excellence, irrespective of the medium, irrespective of the period, irrespective of the rulers, irrespective of the religious protagonists who caused its monuments to be built.

The fountainhead of its artistic expression is (to use Durant's own words) "the tolerance and gentleness of the mature mind, the quiet content of the unacquisitive soul, the calm of the understanding spirit, and a unifying and pacifying love for all living beings"—a philosophy preached not only by the Jain religion, but which is India's cardinal teaching to the world.

The Jain temples of Mount Abu are a symbol and sample of this artistic expression.

Appendices

Explanatory Note
on the Appendices

Three articles written by me have been appended to this book on the *Art Shrines of Ancient India*:

(1) The Siva Sakti theme in Ancient Indian Art
(2) Homage to the Sun in Ancient Indian Art and
(3) Art in Modern India.

Why have I done so?

The article on *Siva Sakti Theme* will enable my readers to have an idea of the concept of *Siva Sakti*, which has inspired a profusion of inspiring sculptures in Ellora, Elephanta, Mamallapuram, Kanchipuram, Badami, Aihole, Khajuraho, Halebid and Madurai, among others. Unless this concept is understood, the enjoyment and appreciation of the sculptures at these places would be incomplete.

The article on *Homage to the Sun* will supplement the list of art shrines with places like Deo in Bihar, Martand in Kashmir, and Modhera in Gujarat.

The article on *Art in Modern India* is intended to indicate that though royal patronage is no longer available to encourage and stimulate artists, craftsmen and sculptors, the Indian artistic heritage bequeathed by our ancestors continues to stimulate and motivate modern Indian artists.

Appendix I

Siva Sakti Theme in Ancient Indian Art

The ancient Indians, while recognising that there exists only one Ultimate Reality, propounded that there are two aspects to it, one static and the other dynamic.

In the Vedas, these two have been mentioned as *Purusha* and *Prakriti*, while in the *Vedanta*, the terms *Brahman* and *Maya* have been used. In *Tantric* philosophy, they became Siva and Sakti.

The indefinable Absolute, in Indian scriptures, has been endowed with the highest of attributes and often converted into a personal God who also exists in the form of the Primeval Father and Mother, ever united, as Kalidasa puts it, as word and meaning.

The highest ideals that the human mind can think of: *Truth*, *Goodness* and *Beauty* were attributed to one's beloved God with the images of Father and Mother.

Mythology and metaphysics, legend and poetry have enveloped these images in the magic of love, devotion and adulation down the ages.

The attributes of Siva, the Auspicious One, include omnipresence, capacity to destroy sin and sorrow, residence in the mountains, possessing a blue neck — for He drank poison out of mercy to save the universe from destruction — a great dancer (*Nataraja*), an ocean of mercy, a doer of good (*Sankara*), residing in everyone as Pure Consciousness, bestowing boundless prosperities on His devotees, while preferring austerity for Himself, the great Ascetic who is also the ideal lover, ever united with His spouse, Sakti.

The concept of Sakti, the divine Mother, like that of Siva, has also evolved over a period of 3000 years. Though the *Vedic* hymns refer to the Goddess in the form of *Rātri,* the Deity of the night, *Durga,* the remover of all the obstacles, and *Sri,* the Goddess of prosperity, the fusion of the various concepts took place only in the *Puranic* period.

The *Devimahatmya* also known as *Chandi* or *Saptasati,* which occurs in the *Markandeya Purana,* is a landmark in the evolution of the concept of Sakti. All branches of learning are Her facets, so too are all the women. She is *Saraswati,* the Goddess of learning, *Lakshmi,* the Goddess of wealth, and *Durga,* the Goddess who helps us to cross the ocean of this phenomenal world.

The vivid images of Siva and Sakti built up by the *Vedic* seers, the teachers of the *Upanishads* and the authors of the epics and *Puranas* were carved in imperishable stone and metal by the great sculptors and craftsmen of India at Badami and Aihole, Mamallapuram and Kanchipuram, Ellora and Elephanta, Khajuraho and Halebid, Tiruvannamalai and Thanjavur, Chidambaram and Madurai, under the patronage of successive rulers like the Chalukyas, Pallavas, Rashtrakutas, Chandellas and Hoysalas, Cholas and Pandyas, and the Nayaks. The rich visual panorama is available for study and interpretation.

The Pallavas (600-850 A.D.) have left valuable archaeological legacies at Mamallapuram and Kanchipuram which contain many sculptural marvels related to the Siva-Sakti theme.

Some very impressive *Siva Sakti* sculptures are also available at the Ellora and Elephanta caves, carved under the patronage of the Rashtrakuta kings during the period (750-975 A.D.).

The Hoysaleswara temple at Halebid in Karnataka, built by the Hoysala rulers between the 12th and 14th centuries, is another magnificent legacy, where the Siva-Sakti theme has been dealt with in ornate detail. It is a double temple, one part dedicated to Siva and the other to Sakti. The whole temple stands on a terrace 5 feet 6 inches in height.

It took 80 years to be built. Though incomplete, it has a breathtaking array of sculptured frescoes.

There are 280 carved figures in the Hoysaleswara temple.

The most important ones include the Divine Couple, Siva and Sakti riding a bull, the dancing Siva trouncing the elephant demon and Nataraja doing the *Tāndava* in unalloyed bliss.

In an essay on the Siva-Sakti theme in ancient Indian art, one cannot omit the famous Meenakshi temple in Madurai (South India). The bulk of the sculptures that can be seen in this temple today were carved during the rule of the Nayaks (1560-1743 A.D.).

A visit to some of these temples would provide a deep spiritual experience, apart from aesthetic appreciation.

Appendix II

Homage to the Sun in Ancient Indian Art

As a life-sustainer of the earth, the sun has been worshipped, the world over, deified as a patent, visible manifestation of the Supreme Power.

In India, during *Sandhya Vandana*,* a mantra is recited, which, when translated means: "The sun is a manifestation of the Supreme, so am I."

The famous *Gayatri mantra* handed to us from the time of *Rigveda* states: "We meditate on the venerable radiance of the deity, Sun. Let it illumine our intellects."

Relics of sun worship exist in such diverse countries like Mexico, Egypt, Iran, Southern Europe, North East America and Australia.

In India, evidence of sun worship during the Indus Valley civilisation is available from the seals and pottery of Harappa, Mohenjodaro, etc.

In Vedic times, the sun was one of the most prominent deities of worship, as is clear from the Vedic hymns which are recited even today by millions everywhere in India.

In the epics, especially the *Ramayana*, sun worship is mentioned. The most famous prayer to the Sun, the *Aditya Hridaya*,

*A devotional ritual performed at dawn, noon and dusk.

which vouchsafes victory in undertakings, and freedom from diseases, was taught by Sage Agastya to Sri Rama for daily recitation, on the eve of his battle with the demon, Ravana.

In this prayer, the Sun is extolled as the primordial deity, with radiant rays, riding in a chariot driven by seven green horses, the resplendent one, the master of the oceans, the ruler of the earth, the destroyer of darkness, the golden-hued giver of light, who rises in the eastern mountains, and sets in the western hills.

Over time, the need was felt to have a visual image of *Sūrya*, the Sun God. The Scythian invaders who brought the Magi Sun priests from Iran were behind the successful spread of this personified cult of sun worship.

Inspired by the imagery of the ancient Indian scriptures, iconographic representation in temples dedicated to the Sun God began.

From the West to the East popular centres of sun worship developed in Multan, Avantipur and Martand (both in Kashmir), Kanauj, Somnath and Konarak and Suryanarkoil (Tamil Nadu).

The first Sun temple was probably built by Samba, son of Krishna, at Multan in Northwest India in the second century A.D.

During the Pratihara period (roughly 8th century A.D.), a Sun temple was built at Osia (Rajasthan).

The most magnificent Sun temples are four in number: the one in Martand in Kashmir; the Modhera temple in Gujarat; Konarak temple in Orissa; and the Deo temple in Bihar.

DEO

The temple at Deo (Bihar) is one of the few temples dedicated to the sun where sun worship is still practised.

Situated off the National Highway No. 2 about 48 miles from Gaya, it is said to have been built by Vishvakarma, the supreme architect at the request of Raja Aila of Prayag (modern Allahabad).

According to legend, the Raja had been cured of leprosy after having washed himself in the muddy waters of a ditch said to have magical properties; whereupon the Sun God appeared before him and ordered that his statue be dug out of the ditch and installed in a temple.

The temple dates back to the 12th century and has bold mouldings, divine figures and carved scrolls on its exterior. However, the circular fiery image of the Sun God stands out amongst the other floral and divine depictions.

The *sanctum sanctorum* houses the solar dieties, Brahma, Vishnu and Mahesh, instead of a Surya image. The most striking feature of this temple is that, unlike traditional Sun temples, it faces west instead of east.

KONARAK

But the most magnificent Sun temple is the one at Konarak, Orissa. It was built by the Ganga Ruler, Narasimha Deva who reigned between 1238 A.D. and 1264 A.D. Konarak is 40 miles by road from Bhubaneshwar, the capital of Orissa, which has an airport and a railhead. From Puri, Konarak is 50 miles by road.

In Sanskrit, *kona* means angle and *arka* means 'Sun'. Thus Konarak means "The Angle of the Sun".

The Konarak temple has been built in the form of a huge chariot of the Sun drawn by seven horses, with 12 beautifully carved wheels, each wheel representing a month of the year and the seven horses presumably symbolising the seven days of the week.

Unfortunately, the temple is in ruins now. Only the *mandapa* remains, the main structure, the *sikhara* falling to pieces. Life-size statues of the Sun God and his charioteer have been carved on three sides of the main temple. By the side of the main edifice stand two elephants and two horses on broad platforms.

The Konarak temple stands in lonely majesty, even in its present state of ruins, on the seashore where the waves roar and produce a sound similar to the *pranava dhwani,* the primeval sound *Aum* paying tribute to the glory of the Sun whose eternal temple is the life lived on earth and whose energy permeates all living beings, vesting them with vitality and procreative power.

MARTAND

Named after the Sun God, the Martand temple was built by King Lalitaditya who ruled Kashmir during the period 699-736 A.D. It is situated at a distance of 5 miles from the town of Anantnag. It has been built on an elevated plateau and overlooks the valley on all sides while the snowclad peaks of the Pir Panjal mountain range stand like sentinels in the background.

The picturesque setting makes the Martand temple a beautiful sight, a worthy monument to the vibrant Sun.

MODHERA

The Modhera temple in Gujarat was built in the eleventh century A.D. Modhera is located at a distance of 60 miles from the city of Ahmedabad, on the left bank of Pushpavati river. The shrine stands on a mound facing east, so that the rising sun shines right through into the sanctum sanctorum.

Today, the Modhera temple is in ruins. The tower is missing, the roofs of the pillared halls are damaged, the images in the niches have gone. Still it remains a monument of masterly majesty.

In the *Araneya subparva* of the *vana parva* of the *Mahabharata* there is a dialogue between Yudhishtira and a Yaksha, indicating the importance attached to the Sun as a symbol of the Divine power, governing the entire solar system.

Unlike other civilisations, which realised the central significance of the Sun and worshipped it, and lapsed into negligence over the centuries, India continues to venerate the life-giving, life-sustaining energy even today in temples, rituals and daily worship which are an integral part of the life of the people, to whom the Sun symbolises sight, light and health.

Appendix III

Art in Modern India

While writing about Art in Modern India, one is instinctively reminded about Kalidasa's famous dictum: "Everything is not good merely because it is old, nor is a work to be rejected merely because it is new."

Tradition and modernity in art are relative terms. Tradition is yesterday's modernity and today's modernity is tomorrow's tradition. The question "Where does modernity begin in Indian Art?" is hence difficult to answer.

The fifteenth century Renaissance in Western art was a watershed, subsequent to which several innovations appeared over a period of five centuries: Baroque, Rococo, Impressionism, Expressionism, Cubism, Surrealism, etc.

The corresponding Indian Renaissance can be deemed to have begun with the Bengal school—a nineteenth century phenomenon which was a reaction of Indian cultural roots to the onset of Western influence.

The giants of Bengal school were: Abanindranath Tagore, Gaganendranath Tagore (Abanindranath's elder brother), Nandalal Bose and the great Rabindranath Tagore himself.

Abanindranath, who may be considered the founder father of Modern Art in India, was born on 7th August, 1871 and died at the ripe age of 80 on December 5, 1951. For about half a century, Abanindranath gave a new direction to Indian painting. He trained a large number of new disciples, including the famous Nandalal Bose.

Abanindranath used to exhort his disciples: "The secret of all art is to efface the hand of effort. The same criterion applies to music as well. A bird in flight does not leave its traces in movement in the air. What is true of music is true of art. They are not made. They are born. Art is a thing of within. Is it only fuel that needs to be set on fire? Only burn yourself and illuminate."

Abanindranath was not a revivalist. In his selection of themes and style he was modern and contemporary. He believed that tradition was like a river. One could drink its water and swim in it but one could not turn it back to its source.

A deep love for Mother India, a respect for traditional folk art, the influence of Japanese prints and Mughal miniatures mingled in the palette of Abanindranath and resulted in paintings of grace, sensitivity and graphic excellence.

If Abanindranath started the trend towards modernity, Gaganendranath and Rabindranath went far ahead, the former imbibing the spirit of Cubism and the latter the essence of Surrealism.

Among the disciples of Abanindranath, the most distinguished was Nandalal Bose, who introduced in his paintings statuesque classical forms. He scrupulously avoided the pretty and the sentimental and emphasised the majesty of form.

Jaimini Roy, again another of Bengal's great painters, drew inspiration from the basic concepts of folk art and developed a characteristic style of his own, marked by simplicity and integration of line and colour though some critics feel that his works are repetitive in style and content.

Amrita Shergil can be deemed to have carried on the torch lit by the pioneers of the Bengal school. Though of mixed Indo-Hungarian descent, she was truly Indian in her approach to painting.

Her schooling in Paris gave her appropriate acumen in the use of colours. She had a sensitive mind and she painted with feeling the sad and suffering profile of India, as she observed them. Amrita Shergil's art was a beautiful blending of the modern techniques of the West with the lyrical mysticism of the East. Amrita unfortunately died at the tender age of 29.

Many paintings of Rabindranath Tagore and Amrita Shergil can be seen at the National Gallery of Modern Art, New Delhi.

Post-independence India has witnessed a mushrooming of artists dabbling in all styles fashionable in the West, but those who stand out are those who have their moorings in Indian soil and Indian people, M.F. Hussain for example.

Hussain stands out not only as the most prolific but also as the most representative of modern Indian art. Krishna Chaitanya, a noted Indian art critic, says that "Hussain's art is mosaic in its psychological import. His presentation condenses many memories, held more by masculine violence than by feminine harmony and its cryptic message has a finality which has to be respected."

Hussain says that his aim in painting is to arrive at a contemporary Indian idiom, find the essential points of art in general and the synthesis with our own thought.

Hussain's advice to Indian artists is: "In our time we have been presented with the folk idiom by Jaimini Roy, the classical aspect by Abanindranath Tagore and George Keyt and the Western technique by Amrita Shergil. The Indian artist has to amalgamate the best points in all these three directions and move forward."

Hussain considers the main source of inspiration to be woman and adds: "*The Indian artistic heritage glorifies woman.*" Though Hussain follows Western art styles like expressionism and cubism, his feel and flavour are Indian, so too are his themes, and the use of bright colours.

Richard Bartholomew observes that Hussain has in his paintings "drawn his imagery from the dance, as performed now and sculpted in stone in temples, the fluid stance and flexed posture being qualities of his figuration. The figure in Hussain's art is a symbol between the illusion of theatre and the idealism of stone sculpture."

It is not possible to deal at length with the other modern painters in this short essay on modern Indian Art, but mention has to be made of Sailoz Mukherjee who had elements of impressionism in his paintings. Biren De and G.R. Santosh with their Tantric inspiration, Satish Gujral, the rusty experimentalist whose art has undergone several changes: of revolt against human barbarity during partition to obsession with tribal imagery, Ramachandran whose main obsession is the human body, Krishen Khanna, the accountant turned artist, Swaminathan with his Upanishadic inspiration, Gaitonde, Raza, Ram Kumar and Akbar Padamse, the mystical landscapist, and F.N. Souza, whose paintings convey torment and sensuality.

There are not many sculptors in modern India, though we are a nation with the richest sculptural heritage in the world. The few worth mentioning are Devi Prasad Roy, Sankho Chaudhry, Dhanraj Bhagat and Amarnath Sehgal.

The varied scenic grandeur of India and the diversity of life lived in snowy hills to barren deserts and the variety of village and folk handicrafts, the myriad variations of dance forms, music and sculpture—all these provide the sensitive artist with perennial sources of inspiration and day by day, increasing numbers of young men and women are coming forward to express, in visual forms, their reaction to them, using styles and techniques which cut across national barriers.

Creativity is related to cultural integrity and it is heartening to find that many of the artists have tried to draw inspiration from indigenous sources. Any modern Indian artist without some link with indigenous roots will not stand the testimony of time. There is, however, great truth in what Biren De once said: "*An important aspect of the artistic tradition of our country has been the healthy acceptance and ultimate assimilation of different aspects of cultural and artistic traditions from outside. In a way, the modern artists of India are carrying on the same.*"

In the past, the best work of painters and sculptors was done in beautifying monasteries and temples. Royal patronage of the past has to be substituted in modern times by state encouragement.

A beginning has been made in setting up state art academies, but much more remains to be done.

Town halls, legislative assemblies, hospitals, banks, railway stations, law courts, government offices, business houses, board rooms, etc. should be decorated with works of Indian artists.

Every estimate for a public building should contain a small provision for decoration with works of art. Scouting and promotion of artistic talent and training in aesthetics should begin at an early age. Then only will we be providing sustenance, motivation and nourishment to Indian art.

Index